Before the "I Dos" & Other Compendiums

Before the "I Dos" & Other Compendiums

Relationship Guides for Dummies

By
S. O. Mukoro

Copyright © 2017 by S. O. Mukoro.

ISBN:	Softcover	978-1-5434-8653-7
	eBook	978-1-5434-8652-0

All rights reserved. No part of this book may be reproduced or transmitted in any form or by any means, electronic or mechanical, including photocopying, recording, or by any information storage and retrieval system, without permission in writing from the copyright owner.

Any people depicted in stock imagery provided by Thinkstock are models, and such images are being used for illustrative purposes only. Certain stock imagery © Thinkstock.

Print information available on the last page.

Rev. date: 07/10/2017

To order additional copies of this book, contact:
Xlibris
800-056-3182
www.Xlibrispublishing.co.uk
Orders@Xlibrispublishing.co.uk

CONTENTS

Introduction vii

Recommendation 1   Dreaming of Genies 1

Recommendation 2   Doubting Thomas's & Jane's 10

Recommendation 3   General Despair 16

Recommendation 4   Your Relationship 21

Recommendation 5   Your ... "It's Complicated" 36

Recommendation 6   Do You Really Want To Marry Me? 47

Recommendation 7   "I Love You" Shouldn't Be A Punchline 53

Recommendation 8   Our Impressions 62

Recommendation 9   What's ... Love? 65

Recommendation 10   Let's Talk About Sex 74

Recommendation 11   Feeding The Wrong Wolf 80

Recommendation 12   And Finally ... Your Love 86

INTRODUCTION

Firstly, every man deserves a woman and every woman deserves a partner. Having said that, no one is perfect, neither is any society. Hence, it is now of appropriate connotation to say in the climate of political correctness and openness to say that every heart deserves a corresponding like-minded heart and vice versa. No marriage is going to be perfect because unfortunately there is no "happily ever after". Fortunately there is however a "happily after".

Marriage is supposed to be wonderful, should be deeply satisfying and mutually fulfilling.

Getting married should be easiest of dreams and decisions we should ever have to make. However, there is that niggling doubt, those fears, and banes we humans always have, that we are forced to, at times to attend to. We all have expectations and yearnings that we cannot deny or fulfil but fortunately, there is also LOVE.

We are flesh, feeling bubbling mass of erroneous and intricate emotions, us humans. We have the need to analyse our doubts, give in to fear, pray to hope and lament in despair. Who could blame us? Just a small percentage of us are sure they never have to deal with such problems. The rest of us feel that when we have to take that plunge into the matrimonial world, we should do it half blindfolded. This book is a relationship guideline for those percentages of us, the girlfriends or fiancées, the boyfriends or grooms who need to be at least fifty to ninety percent sure.

Take it to heart, but do not set your prayers by it. Consider, that "it is better to wait long, than to marry wrong". Your heart is the true gift you will ever need to be sure about that person standing next to you.

Before we get started ...

*"Marriage is not about finding the right person
as it is about being the right person"*

Marriage is a matter of LAW. Sometimes religious law or society's law. Marriage is also on occasion, a question of expediency but fortuitously it is also a matter of LOVE.

Certain early cultures used edicts and directives to govern our primitive emotions the while advent of the church laid down early laws governing the pursuit of happiness to produce a certain holiness in our lives.

Until the end of the 17th century, marriages could be held, anywhere provided they were conducted before some sort of ordained minister. This unfortunately encouraged secret and bigamous marriages. It also allowed wealthy males to marry under-aged partners.

Thankfully, with the change of laws in the 1750s, 1830s, the 1929 minimum age act and the latest 2013 same sex law, marriage has become a more convenient institution and definitely a real bond to achieve.

Though marriage is the rule that civilisation has chosen to govern our sexual ideals, these days, some marriages are all about motivational contracts, whether arranged or not. Every now and then, on occasion it will have something to do with turning a profit. Be it money, property, prestige or some other motive.

If you haven't yet and are about to get married you may not yet realize that marriages are important and the experience you about to undertake will be as eye opening to you as you ever thought possible. In a true marriage, you will experience both the amazing and the hard choices of married life. Marriage eliminates loneliness, opens you to challenges, both decent and severe. It will mature you and if willing through your union, you will be able to produce miniature carbon copies of yourself.

The union of man and woman or any gay couple should be a personal indenture and not a communal rapport. It ought to be a good relationship and environmental contentment in which to live harmoniously, bearing and raising children, as well as definitely exerting an essential influence on the common good.

THE FOUR "SUPPOSEDLY" GROUND RULES FOR ANY MARRIAGE

1) INTEGRITY

Marriage should be a bond and when partners become one, they move through the challenges of life with integrity. Integrity should be owned and sometimes learned. Learn to act well, give, and receive as you wish those unknown should do to you. It is the ingredient to a fruitful and happy marriage.

2) FAITH

Marriage is designed for faith. Faith that is assaulted by temptation nearly every minute from so many directions. Marriage should give us support to defeat any temptation by engaging in a deep satisfying love. A faith that gives and receives physically, emotionally and spiritually.

3) **GENUINE LOVE**

Love will always be a part of us. It will never leave or forsake us. Even the most evilest person has some spark of love in them, though their version of love is slightly obtuse and askew. Love between partners should be unconditional, with that, contentment follows, and exultation abounds.

4) **RESPECT**

The natural order of things is that wives submit to the authority of their husbands. The truth for both husband and wife should be to submit to each other's authority wherever necessary. They should both honour each other, as they would like to be honoured.

SOME FACTS YOU NEED TO KNOW ABOUT MARRIAGE:

EARLY MARRIAGE: The utmost known risk factor for divorce is marrying young. Teenagers who marry are more likely to divorce than people who marry in their twenties or later.

INTRODUCTION: Despite the romantic fact, that there is Love at first sight or the simplest notion that people meet, fall in love through chance or fate, there is plenty of evidence that suggests that these days, social networks is becoming the major influence in bringing together couples with similar interests and backgrounds. That does not mean friends, family members or acquaintances are not also likely to introduce you to a future partner.

CONNEXIONS: Opposites may attract, yes. All the same, people who have similar values, backgrounds and life goals are more liable to have a successful marriage than couples who are very different in their experiences and communal associations. That does not mean they may not live harmoniously as married couples but the better the background the healthier the marriage.

SINGLE PARENTING: Having a child out of wedlock reduces the chances of ever marrying. At least for women. Weirdly, men have an appreciably better chance of marrying if they are a single parent. It is the least desirable characteristic a potential mate can possess next to the lack of ability to hold a steady job.

TRIAL MARRIAGE: Cohabitating before marriage is not 100% effective as a precursor to marriage. Couples who cohabitate before marriage are likely to experience a host of problems that may lead to marital conflict, marital unhappiness, and maybe eventually divorce. This is because it is likely that some — especially younger couples - of the differences in the characteristics of people do not manifest during cohabitation. The negative effects of cohabitation on future marital success propagate, as living together becomes a habitual experience. This does not mean that the cohabitating experience is a bad idea, it just means that both parties must be sincere in their actions when living together. For example; if you fart during the brushing of your teeth, do not hide the fact to your partner. Knowing his or her faults, for better or worse before marriage is a favourable factor, not a bad one.

AFFLUENCE: The healthier the marriage, the best it does economically. It has been proven that marriage aids in generating income and fortitude. Men become more productive and women become more nurturing and happier. The social criteria needed to encourage martial health, productivity, beneficial comportment and the accumulation of wealth. Wealthy couples have been known to attribute their happiness to their collective specialization and the pooling of their resources. Families are more likely to be monetarily sympathetic to married people, possibly because families consider marriage a more permanent and binding union.

EDUCATION: People whom are analogously educated are more likely to marry than those who are of a higher or a lower level of education. They are also less prone to divorce. There is an erroneous but corresponding belief that women marry their less learned peers. That is not true. The gender gap in education may be difficult for learned women to find their comparably erudite partner. We can already see this with African-American female graduates, who significantly outstrip their African-American male counterparts.

SEX: Can it be true that married couples have more fun emotionally and physically after sex? The answer is YES. Not a definite yes but a more satisfying yes. Married couples have a more satisfying sex life, contrary to popular belief. They have higher levels of sexual gratification and sexual activity than other couples. This is as a result of a higher level of commitment between couples in marriage and therefore a greater sense of trust, security, and better communication between spouses.

HERE ARE SOME TINY DETAILS YOU SHOULD BE AWARE OF AND NOT MISS:

1) Trust, trust, trust. Should be the known moniker of your lives together. Things will change over time for no apparent reason, it cannot be helped and you will both be faced with challenges both known and unknown. It would be best that trust is the bona fide backbone of your relationship. If your partner feels a specific way about some nonsense you do not understand, then trust that he or she does. It is certainly not their fault they do not think the same way as you do. The same goes for you. Your feelings no matter what they are, are neither right nor wrong.

2) Do not get jealous. Trust each other's feelings. Your partner may have a wandering eye but as long as he comes home to you, you feel no jealousy. Good for you. Jealousy gets you nowhere. Unless you have cause to.

3) Will you be sexually comfortable offering and accepting your partners love? Do either of you feel your love for each other? If you don't, what are you doing together?

4) Are either of you satisfied with the frequency of your lovemaking? Do you both share the desired levels? Are each of you matched? How often will you be having sex? Every two days, every day, every weekends, every other weekend, Every Tuesday on even numbered days or when the mood overcomes you?

5) Do either or you want kids? How important is it to either of you? How many and when in your life do you wish to have them? Will a child compromise your ideals or your status? Have you even discussed it?

6) How will you tolerate your partner's obnoxious habit? His or her bad diet, his or her smoking, or their collection of star wars memorabilia etc.?

7) If you are both religious but of different dominations, which one do you both pledge to or let your children ascribe to? Do you ascribe to both i.e. Catholic and Synagogue? If not, do you decide by affiliation?

8) Are your friends conducive to your lifestyles? Should you both be more socially inclined or cut down on your social commitments? Do you worry about your communal or office status?

WHAT NOT TO DO IN A MARRIAGE:

Vent Your Anger: When in a marriage you have to compromise and subjugate many of your own needs and feelings to those of others. Many divorces can be traced to the fact that one partner learned as a family rule or a training tool never to express feelings on the belief it makes them look weak or for some other reason. Fair enough. Find some outlet where you can express your anger somehow. Join a kick boxing class. Climb a hill and yell at the sunrise, something to let go of the built up anger within you. Do not do it when surrounded with family.

Avoid Psychosomatic Games: When in conflict do not try to inflict a loss on your partner so that you can claim victory. It does not resolve problems and rather prevents couples from becoming closer. Try some other outlet, if that does not help join a chess club, a spin class or some other activity outside your comfort zone.

Sending Mixed Messages: Communications with two meanings, not only contradict each other, they are troublesome to interpret and hurt the matrimonial relationship. For example, you have just had an argument and you are mad at your spouse but she or he asks you if you are mad and you retort with harsh voice "No". Well my friend, your actions speak louder than words.

Not Listening: You should make an effort to pay attention to your partner's comments. Listen and be empathetic, even if he or she is talking about Curling, knitting, or especially the most boring subject that you can make neither heads nor tails of.

Avoid Resolving Problems: Discuss ideas on how to improve your marriage and resolve any pending issues for a healthier and sustainable marriage.

Criticize Your Spouse: Not many people, including your family understand the value of your spouse until it is too late. They end up criticizing him or her and making you jump on the bandwagon. You don't listen or share your thoughts with him or her, especially when he or she has been making a mess of things lately. It is easy to slip away to the comfortable zone where you take your partner for granted. It is best you always listen without criticizing. Be there when they need you. None of this "Oh he or she won't be mad" or "To hell with her or him". Never take your partner for granted. Try to let them know how much they mean to you. Trust me. After all, you did see something in them that made you want to marry him or her.

Lie: Yes, we know marriage is a compromise, but lying about some menial tasks or even big crazy tribulations is not worth it. Lying at any time is a bad idea. Especially if you are not good at it. It has the added effect of coming back at you.

PREMARITAL QUESTIONS YOU NEED TO DEAL WITH BEFORE MARRIAGE:

1. What are your combined or individual pursuits?

   This has to do with relationship stability. Fostering your own individual interests while also taking care of your relationship. When love is new, couples typically want to spend as much time together as possible and prefer to do things together. As the relationship matures, it's natural for this intense togetherness to taper and for individual interests to emerge.

   While you're busy preparing to get married, it should be important to carve out some time for you and your spouse/partner to answer the above questions and share your responses with each other. Look for areas of understanding and overlap with any differences that you think might cause some problems in the future.

2. What are your expectancies concerning about household maintenance responsibilities?

   You may not know it but many resentments build when a spouse feels there is an unfair distribution of household chores. Couples expect a certain amount of collaboration between them. It is important to discuss equality when it comes to the regular running of household chores.

3. You both have Careers, and financial expenditure, so what do you expect regarding your spending and savings?

   Money will always be a delicate matter for couples. In no time, it could become a sticky point no matter how much money a couple earns. Problems arise over different spending habits, purchases, distribution, career priority over the relationship and family compromise and mutual understanding are the goals when discussing these sensitive issues. However, if you never address these problems and presume that you and your other half are on the same page, you will undoubtedly be blind-sided at some point.

4. Your leisure times, how do you expect to spend them?

   Part of maintaining a healthy marriage is having fun activities together. Creating new adventures together when you get bogged down by the stress of life is a compound result when dealing with stress. Break out of the rut of your day-to-day to day routine and spend it together. You don't need to be totally compatible on this point, but it should be important to find some reasonable hair loose moments but if you do have different expectations about what "relaxing" or "having fun" will look like then go for it.

5. What are your hopes regarding your friends?

   Couples differ in their appeal to spend time with friends. They each have individual friends as well as other couples you enjoy socializing with together. On occasion one partner has a stronger need to maintain their friendships and spend time outside the relationship to socialize. In this case, one of the partners might feel insecure and even jealous.

HOW CAN YOU SHOW YOUR LOVE FOR YOUR PARTNER?

From my perspective and life/love experiences, the majority of sane individuals understand Love's characteristics and attributes. They can be shown in many different ways.

Smile: Smile goes a long way in any situation. A look into your spouse's eyes while you smile lets them know that they are of great value to you. Both male and female lovers like it when their spouses smiles at them and tells them that they love them.

Turn a Normal Day into a Celebration: An act of random partying is a call for genuine festivity. Motivate your partner and your marriage by having a spur-of-the-moment special day. Take him or her out for a dinner or lunch when she or he least expects it or have a wedding anniversary on a day that is not unique in any way to you both. Call it Couples or Jubilee day, in honour of your mate. It will double the value of your marriage and boost your partner's ego. He or she will want to continue caring for you and make sure you know it.

Add Some Spice In Your Lives: At times couples become complacent. And why not, the chase is over. There is no longer any need to put on a show or try as hard as they can to win his or her heart. Couples tend to lack the effort to motivate some life back into the marriage. They should sit down and list ten or twenty things that would like to improve. One or both partners should arrange impromptu date nights. Date nights that should come with strings. Prepare this as if this was your first or second date. Anticipate your luck by hoping for a sexual encounter.

Knowing Them: You know your partner best. Think what you would want done for yourself if the roles were reversed. Even the cheesiest gift, poem, or act can be romantically profound.

RECOMMENDATION 1

DREAMING OF GENIES

"For your ideal partner to be real and for he or she to meet your fantasy parameters you'd have to be living on Fantasy Island"

Our dreams and hopes lie in all of us. It speaks to us, guides us, and in some extreme cases, rules us. It happens while we sleep, drink, shit, dance or wait and when we least expect it. It can stir, open its jaws and scream to high heaven and / or devour us. There are no two ways about it and never an easy way through it.

As humans, we do our colossal best to see through them, even beyond implacable times. Why? Because, it is our undisputable right to indulged in our dreams, our wishes, and our prayers. What choice do we have? Our dreams are the foundation of our finest moments, be it achievements or our monument to the joys of love but also they are the clarity of hatred and the ecstasy of grief. They come alive within us and put us through rigorous Calisthenics, but as long as we are content with the result, we dream of living them even if the choices we make displeases us.

Our dreams and hopes are etched into our psyche. They sometimes take the form of our subconscious desires and wishes. Unlike Santa's "naughty or nice" lists, our lists of dreams and wishes determine our choices. They inform us when we should turn right or question whether you go to that party alone, with friends, or not at all. Or query, the validity of why we should or shouldn't ask her or him out or quibble whether that boy or chick is fine or not or hope if your ideal partner should at least have green eyes and look like Pete Sampras or Ryan Reynolds, or maybe she should be like Brook Shields or Maria Tomei.

Our wish lists are endless and could be any number of things, but most relate to our spouses appearance, hopefully internally and outwardly. We all are fussy, even if we do not realise it and realistically, we cannot always have what we want. Our imagination and desires has already been imprinted into our minds and for all that is holy it has forever tickled our fantasy.

When we begin our dating life, we all begin with a profile. How she or he would look like. What colour her eyes would be. Does he have nice teeth? Will he be willing to stay an extra hour from that important meeting to make you smile? Will she be amused if you made a fool of yourself? Will he wait in the rain to walk you home? Will she accept your failure and stand by you? Does he look good in a tuxedo? Is she fat, average, or lean? Is he chubby or athletic enough? Is she smart, is he poor, does he have any genetic anomaly that would preclude him from giving you babies? God, there are so many aspirations of our wishes we cannot seem to think straight at times.

Ok I might be a bit presumptuous. This is not for you. You have already found your ideal partner or you should have if you are reading this. The point is, we all have clear definitions on what we want, but do we necessarily know what we need. Dreams of couples should be an electric space between them.

Regarding marriage, it is never going to be that simple. How our ideal mate should be number one on our lists of dreams and hopes. We all believe that we deserve our ideal partner. Our nature is to hope for the optimum effect of happiness. To plan for the best of action that gets us to those few steps before the altar and that is why we have dreams. Unfortunately, we rarely do find him or her, even when we are looking hard at the ideal partner straight in the eye. The blinders around our eyes due to our dreams, prevents us.

Women have a great insight into this because they have dreams as early as their first menstrual cycle and even long before that. I would venture to say as early as they first understood how the birds and bees function.

Laura, a friend of mine conjured her dream when she first became a flower girl at an uncle's wedding. She was five. Her dream included her first kiss, her first date, first boyfriend, her wedding dress and of course, how her husband would look beside her in their wedding album.

Some of us have hopes that do not manifest until after a disastrous marriage or even a good one. They evolve over time and we never know what we want until we genuinely need it.

'Akin' my friend's sister's husband did not have a dream, just the hope that he never needed until he ritually proposed to his long-term girlfriend. His dream was quite different. It detailed the number of women he would sleep with before his big day. The score of how much each of them faired in the looks department and how good the sex was. It was not until he was on his bachelor party that he scribbled his hope concerning his ideal mate.

This can be the difference between a prospective male and female spouse.

Granted, these are poor examples of the difference between Men on Mars and Women on Venus. In any case, it is a forgone conclusion that the occasion to make a dream come true almost never arises for men, while women have theirs locked in their heads and are always on the lookout. Even if they would never admit it.

Money, height, blue eyes, and six-packs are insignificant when compared to courage, openness, conviction, and passion. Many of these qualities make quite a dent in the hopes of women.

In my twenties, I was dumped by my girlfriend at the time, because I did not meet the set criteria she had set for herself. She envisioned something I would not be for a million years and went through a well-worn list of potential partners until she thought she had met her dream match. She was over the moon, smug, happy and definitely looking forward to her promising future. It did not last. Three months after the happiest day in her life, her husband became a brute and became someone she least expected. A year later, she filed for divorce. This is an extreme example about that partner across from us, looking at us with those deep-felt soulful eyes and whose touch you crave. It also highlights the danger with our fantasy dreams. Never take your eyes off that dream of yours but listen to that heart of yours. It should be at least your guideline on how you should expect your life partner to be.

Our dreams and hopes are our fantasies and fortunately a guideline. If you have a preference, that should not mean you should treat them lightly. Our hopes are like, wishes attached to minefields. In this day of social media and irascibility, we should learn how to defuse and/or separate them into tangible parts and isolate the real from the imagined.

Unfortunately or fortunately, depending on your nature we need to pin our herromantic hopes on someone. An attentive, appreciative, and faithful man or woman could teach their partner a few new things. They may not be for the better or for the worse, but they will be lessons learnt.

If we can manage to connect, at least half of the characteristics of what are on our dream list with our ideal mate then we have succeeded where many others have failed.

Our dream lists is supposed to be made up of qualities of what we most desire, a guarantee against the heartbreaks we might face. Our hopes are not contracts, because in love, life and marriage, unlike death and taxes, there are no guarantees

DREAMS & HOPES OF MEN:

FAMILY:

Believe it or not, all men crave to have the family life. Marriage is the beginning of that family but it is also a life-long commitment. Some men hate growing up, while others cannot wait to grow up. Marriage provides the prospect to selflessly grow to serve your partner and when able, your children. Marriage for men is more than a physical union, it is also a materialistic and emotional union.

COHESION:

Men more than women love the notion of togetherness. When a man marries, that "Two become one" notion becomes a bond like no other. Just like a footballer on the field with his teammates ready to confront the braves of the opposing team. It gives or shows men they have a life partner, a team-builder, behind them. A strong position to be in as he moves through the trials of life.

PURITY:

Purity is a requisite design in pairing, especially when it comes to marriage, according to the primitive ape hindbrain in men's mind. Maybe it is because from long ago in their genes, they have been programmed to be under assault by the next roving virile nascent or alpha male. The constant bombarding assault of the senses, breeds jealousy, and temptation that reeks from every direction.

The marriage bond gives them the support to defeat whatever enticement or resentments they might have. That sense of a deep, satisfying embracing love is more often than not a cleanser that washes away those pesky sensations or beliefs. A true love that gives and receives in every which way, physically, emotionally, and spiritually. In this precept, the adage *"Love Conquers All"* is very apt.

PARENTING:

It is truly a blessing when a child is introduced into the family unit. Nevertheless, the effects are always staggering. No matter the way, the child was brought in, by birth or adoption. Most men dream to be fathers. Not only because they feel more manly to have produced a child, but also that they could now feel certain that their family will continue long after they're gone. They love being progenitors. The absence of a father can cause in their child mental and behavioural disorders as well as criminal activity and substance abuse. However, if children are raised in a healthy marriage, they get a front row seat to see and experience the lasting benefits of strong family bond.

LOVE:

Marriage is designed to mirror our Creator's unconditional love for us, that may be why Love has no reason and no rhyme. A kind of love that some men mirror which will never leave them or at best make them forsake their partners. At least, in realistic stable conditions. People often believe that they are in love when they actually are not. All the same, when a woman loves a man with that unconditional love, contentment and it is reciprocated, joy flourishes.

DREAMS & HOPES OF WOMEN:

CHILDHOOD WISHES:

Believe it or not, every girl has had a dream since childhood about getting married to the prince charming of her dreams. This dream stays with her until the day she walks down the aisle and perhaps long after. She would have thought of her wedding day, how it will be, what her wedding dress will be, the dress her maid of honour will be wearing, the flower girl, the rings even how her wedding cake will be and mounted. This is ingrained into the minds of most girls and held in the fantasy cerebellum region of every woman. The wedding day, is a boundless theme for many girly conversations, which is why many romance movies revolve around the details of weddings and how they get there.

EMOTIONAL STABILITY:

Most women dislike being without a stable situation and / or a serious allegiance. More often than not, men freak-out when their partners make propositions that end in marriage. Some women too, get all anaemic and mawkish when it comes time to commit. They need authentic financial, and emotional security. Fortunately, more and more women are very independent these days. They do not need a man to provide any kind of pecuniary or emotive security. Unfortunately, more than ninety percent of women are emotional beings, they crave marriage and an emotional partnership that requires a partner who will stand by them come rain, sleet, sunshine and snow.

PATERNAL PRESSURE:

Many women, especially the young successful ones, face a lot of parental pressure to get married. Specifically, from their mothers. And, they need the deed done ASAP! Some parents can be exceedingly nagging about their daughter's wedding, which adds to the pressure. Whilst, parents of men are not too concerned about their son getting hitch, until the time is right. This may be due to women maturing much more rapidly than men do or because emotional astuteness comes faster to a woman than it does to a man. Consequently, the need for marriage is much more prudent and forced upon them by parents before they are willing to commit. Parents fear that as their daughter gets older, she might turn to an old shrew or be unattractive to entice a groom who is good enough for her and able to provide them with grand kids.

PEER PRESSURE:

The bouquet at any wedding is the highlight of a single woman's wedding experience. There is always a single woman waiting to catch that bouquet at the wedding. This is because there is a significant amount of communal pressure among ladies to get married. A single girl who has friends who are married feels a mounting pressure more than a single guy does to get married. There will always be a relative or friend who will thrust the inconsistency of her solitary nature, including pointing out how it may be too late for her to find a decent guy. Certain relatives will become cupids and tire out a woman with their constant matchmaking schemes with some fella or the other.

TESTIMONY TO THE WORLD:

Marriage, for a woman is not purely a pledge to a man, but an unrestricted declaration of love to the public. Exchanging vows and admitting to the world and in the presence of her loved ones that this person is "Her's". It is a unique experience every girl wishes to have. It is her declaration to the world that she has finally found love and wishes to have a beautiful life ahead with the mate standing by her side.

MATERNAL INSTINCT:

Women by nature have what is intuitive known as a maternal instinct. Could it be because of "God's Curse" or because in prehistoric times, women stayed near to the caves or huts with the kiddies tending to their safety, while the men hunt? Maybe, maybe not. At any rate, it may be one of the reasons women tend to marry faster than men. Conceiving a child is a necessary step in heightening that instinct which becomes more and more problematic for a woman as she ages. It is not a very congenial notion for a woman to have a child at the age of forty-two, because it is demanding to handle children with advanced years in tow.

RECOMMENDATION 2

DOUBTING THOMAS'S & JANE'S

> *"My heart is the only thing I know well enough to think about. It can sometimes lead to complications"*

You find something strange on your skin, should you ignore it and go to the beach or see a physician? Your answer proves that your do not have to ignore your doubts. Doubts do not go away on vacation. Deciding whom, when and even if to marry are decisions we all are often encumbered with. This usually is accompanied by uncertainty and stress. The scepticisms and nervousness during the preceding steps of marriage are all big decisions, and who could blame you. Big decisions follow us through life, love and happiness, and no wonder.

Is your soon-to-be significant other, a good person? Is he or she worthy of you and the hassle of married life? Do you want to have kids? How will your work life be? What kind of person are you marrying? Does his or her family like you? What colour will the drapes be in your home? Who will do the dishes, or do you take the kids to school on alternative days, who will do Tuesday and who will do Thursdays? These and many other questions will rattle through your brain. Big and minor decisions that will affect you all the time, creating hesitations and flawed ambiguity.

Doubt, uncertainty and that feeling of not knowing does not necessarily mean that there is a problem. Such feelings could be a great insight toward an intuitive certainty. A belief in a long marriage with shared decisions might dampen those doubts.

Sometimes doubts about marriage reflect the fragile nature of the premarital relationship or factors that predispose divorce. Like a spouse brought up by divorced parents or a single one, or one with a difficult personality.

Noticing body signals can help you notice those doubts. It could also aid in avoiding getting involved with a harsh, insalubrious lover or be curious enough to chase a decent spouse whom at first did not seem your type or is your type but has atrocious manners.

Being sceptic is normal. Having what is usually termed *"Second thoughts"* or *"Cold feet"* is common and not benign. You have to know yourself, trust your partner and the relationship better than anyone else, if you are nervous to the changes you are about to undergo. Address it, talk about it, and try to work on it and hope they have been resolved before the big day.

Your inner voice tends to whisper to you via the pit or knot in your stomach, sleepless nights, whispers in your head, Goosebumps, or any feeling of tension you are having. Pay particular attention to what you are nervous about and explore it.

THOUGHTS YOU MAY WANT TO CONSIDER:

- Having unrealistic expectations and believing in a fairy-tale marriage can lead you to disillusionment.
- Do not ignore that little voice or warnings in your bond. Ignoring the red flags may potential cause you a lot of anguish in the time ahead.
- Never have large problems or issues before the big day, they will likely be the same problems and issues you will have throughout your marriage.

- Before getting married make sure the issues of having children for the right reasons have been resolved.

DOUBTS IN MEN

I once asked my Dad, a successful businessman, when he finally knew what to do with his life.

My Dad replied 'Still waiting. When I do, I'll let you know'

An ambiguous answer, I know. All the same, when it comes to Love and relationships, we all despair about things we cannot change and have doubts about everything else. Who we are with, why are we with them, are just transitions, or phases we all go through. Just like some of the choices, we make when we were young. The girlfriend we had when we were seventeen did not make much sense to the one we had at say twenty-four.

We are simply different people through the various stages of our lives.

- Doubts are a certainty of life. We cannot fight it, nor should we try. If at all possible, it should be embraced, cornered, and drowned like the damn sonofabitch it is. At best, the doubts that formulate in our minds or actions, the doubts that we experience can ultimately lead to positive and creative changes. Having said that, when the changes we envision does not happen, it can hollow us out from within. Pray, it doesn't come to that.
- When it concerns our future spouse, doubt will always linger and possibly play a significant part in your day-to-day lives. You have to figure out how significant it will be. A major part or a tiny insignificant part.
- If you have a thrilling life with friends, co-workers and relations but you dread the prospect of life with her: Sir ... you know what to do. Move on.

I know this may not be a prospect of life you were expecting but when a relationship stales like bread, then you have a problem. A healthy relationship should smell like fresh baked bread. It should be always be in the process of baking bread.

- Most doubts that stem from men's mind are sometimes about appearance, loss of hair or Libido. When men reach a certain age, they think about that penile clock. Men do not think about it much because they think they have all the time in the world, as long as their cock can stand erect. Men can easily put a snooze button on their ticking telomere clock.
- Family obligations, envy or pressure can prompt a desperation in men that can turn out to be catastrophic but sometimes worthwhile.
- Men who search for partners are less frantic than women who are. A man can buy a wife or even rent one. It would be a cold day in heaven if a woman could do that. That is unless she is wealthy or has no qualms.
- Most men live in the now. Their doubts for the ideal mate would include her knowing how to cook his favourite meal, will she have sex whenever he wants, will she be a respectful and supporting wife and could she maintain her beautiful at all times.

Please be careful, single women resonate with the ideals that the right man for them is actually out there somewhere. While men echo with the fact that the woman across them, on yet another date, is there only for privilege of sleeping with them.

DOUBTS IN WOMEN

It is normal to get jittery around the time proceeding your wedding day. Women envision a man who would lift them out of their loneliness, transport them to that magical place and when he fails to appear or live up to the expectation, they will "settle" for the nearest or closest match. However, jitters or cold feet around your wedding day may be cause to call the whole thing off. As a fan of positive affirmation as well as being a hopeless romantic, the bandwagon of the concept of slippery ideals can be demanding and full of unrealised fantasies. It just might be all in your mind, everyone has doubts. It is on par for a marriage.

Here are some doubts that might be causing those jitters.

- Family commitments, resentment, and pressure can prompt a desperation in women that can turn out to be catastrophic and dangerously irresponsible even if it sometimes produces a true desire.
- As far as the interest with your future spouse, doubt will always dawdle. The bucolic promise of happiness will not happen if you continue to dwell on your doubts. Depending on your zeal, this doubt will possibly play a significant part in your regular lives. If you have major concerns you have to figure out how significant it should be. A foremost part or an inconsequential one. If you are undecided, then do something about it.
- "Should I get married to him or her?" will be a constant question you ask yourself, and possibly close friends. If your answer is, "I think I should" rather than "Maybe I shouldn't", then you had better do some serious thinking. Just asking the question is cause to re-evaluate not only your answer but also your relationship.
- He does not care about wedding planning or any of that sissy stuff. Your wedding should be a unique thoughtful and personal event you both have to share, regardless of his interests. Indifference to your wedding is a red flag and so is hyperactively focusing on it. Your wedding day is an important event to you and your spouse, not the event itself.
- You tend for no reason at all find yourself crying, like all the time. You cry when you are stressed, when you are

contented, in your doctor's office, when shopping for your wedding dress, listening to the words of Crazy Love, etc. then something is wrong about your relationship. You may be in a funk or something else. It's a tough thing to figure out when big life changes make you emotionally unsure of yourself

- Rarely hanging out with your spouse is a sure indicator of your doubts about him or her. If it is not a long distance relationship but for other reasons, like his or her friends or because of his attitude you prefer to keep your distance, then you have doubts that figure into your intentions about him or her.
- Your partner has become a belligerent puerile lout.
- You would rather be single than deal with the prospect of being married.
- It is plain and simple. You really do not want to get married. You dislike the idea of the pressure from your partner, family, and society. Despite your idea of not being loved or your desire to enjoy the pleasures your friends get out of their relationships.

Martial satisfaction, engagement, history of parental divorce, premarital cohabitation, and neuroticism significantly plague women with premarital doubts. A precursor to doubt is every so often during a couple's engagement.

RECOMMENDATION 3

GENERAL DESPAIR

"Despair tends to take the simplest possible view. As soon as you start to scratch the surface of any predicament, it starts to become more and more complicated"

You are where you thought you would never be. You thought if you did everything right, follow the rules, be a good person, everything would be just fine. You have the right man or woman, he or she is attractive, passable and well-to-do. What can go wrong?

Well sorry friend, misery and ineptitude go hand in hand with life. If you aren't feeling heartache about someone then you are truly not in love with that person. Misery and despair is your friend until it is not. Despair is the fire where all true feelings come from, it is like wet ash clogging our oesophagus and stifling our breath. A nice, stable relationship can at times be just that wheezy and intense, until it is not. Love and pain do sometimes go with passion and conflict. Like bacon and eggs. You really do not want to go without the other.

When we think of marriage, we think of love, compassion, friendship, and happiness. Living in today's time is difficult even when we do not think of marriage. Culture is this very minute dictating a much bigger role in marriages, which causes so many hardship aspects not only between couple's especially young spouses, but also among families.

As a goal, we all seek the paths to walk that limits or ultimately avoids the outcome of despair. With women, despair can come from any direction.

A friend of a friend once told me of this beautiful successful lady who was exceedingly proud of herself and her beauty. She saw herself as better than average to any woman and most men in her social circle. Moreover, she was right. Every other week she would be asked out and every other month she would receive a proposal for marriage. She rejected all comers, ignoring her biological clock. Thinking to herself, that they did not deserve her or that they could not handle her or her explicit particular needs. Eventually, it reached a point when she got older, when her beauty was not all that special. Her breasts became less perky, crow's-feet started appearing on her eyes, and the proposals became few and far between, until they finally stopped. In desperation, she accepted a proposal that was obnoxiously incongruent to her idea of a happy married life and committed suicide four months after pledging her wedding vows.

The moral of this mastoidial story is to not look a gift horse in the mouth. Or better still, it is wise to consider any proposals and not just reject them out of hand. This applies to men too. Do not lose hope thinking you are better than others are because you will find out, probably the hard way, that you are not.

Sometimes, it is not the biological clock women or men have to be desperate about. More often than not, it is about some other factor. One of those facts are children. If they are young, their itinerary from waking in the morning and getting them safely into bed will be an ongoing day-to-day crisis routine, which will be set in stone. Who would blame a man or a woman searching for that kind-hearted eager mate for some relief.

The sexual relationship between engaged couples on the verge of marriage should be more than "just sex". When accepting a proposal, it is a foregone conclusion that committing to a sexual partner who will continue to make that union alive and complete must be a high point. The vows - sacred or not - you intend to accept will commit you to a sexual fidelity that should make your love grow. An Oxytocinchemical secure attachment that ensures a tolerance and expectancy with our partner's differences. Regrettably, this is not always be the case. Either spouse will not only fantasise but also immerse himself or herself in a relationship with a lover who will be able to fit his or her schedule into either partner's rather inflexible parameters. And when they can't, the next Josephine or Joe who is barely hanging on themselves and is desperate enough to fill his or her days, could be solicited to take up the mantle of being the other lover. This undoubtedly is concern for great despair.

Hope and trust allows us to feel a sexual connection to our partner's fulfilment. On the flip side, there is a classification of people whom I like to categorise as *"Sexual Dissociates"*. These individuals are inexpressive and contemptuous when it comes to sex. They appear bored and unattached when making love. They mechanically view the quality of a sexual encounter as "Just sex", a futile humdrum that needs doing. Such dissociative partners avoid kissing and other intimate actions. Sometimes they seek sexual gratification elsewhere like a red zone joint or striptease club. Of course, there could be another reason for this behaviour, such as a low libido or the loss of interest or some other reason but more often than not, these spouses opt for porn use, masturbation or hookers than a real coupling interaction. Preoccupied sexuality is anxiously wrong and as children we have been intermittently ingrained with the thought it is just plain inappropriate. This does not mean that sexual dissociates are dysfunctional, they could always move to the other end of the spectrum and develop a productive pattern that encourages affection, cordiality and a renewed nourishment for an intimate connection. Unfortunately, not all partners make the adjustment. They develop a miserable precedent of dismissal and uneasiness. A sexual dissociate partner could be a cause for great despair to his or her companion, especially if the mate is a very sexual and precocious individual.

Another factor that can cause desperation is your job. Your employment can deeply affect your desperation. Loving your work is a great factor when tying the knot. If you love it too much you might as well be married to it. If you do not, then its best you seek a confidant in the form of a marriage.

In this climate of social media, our judgements and etiquette have been obscured and our valued views and opinions have been replaced by digital and analogue perspectives. This could be another source of desperation. We oftentimes think of how our relationship would be viewed in the virtual world. Projecting your aspirations for a meaningful relationship should not have to be a forum for public opinion. Imagine your partner seeking dates online and accepting them but does not follow through. Would you consider it as an honest harmless vice or a disrespectful one? Does it suggest an uncaring or uncommitted relationship? Dating sites are genuinely a Godsend, but an abuser of such sites is possibly a porn addict or a craver of attention or perhaps someone so insecure with their sexuality and the relationship they are currently having or not having, that they are in need of constant erotic reassurance. In my belief, once in a fruitful relationship has been established such online dating sites should be a think of the past.

Despite everyone telling you that your relationship despair will pass, that everything will be ok, and that you need to just hang in there, it does not help. You want to scream and tear your hair out. They - your family, friends, and acquaintances - do not understand and will never. Do you address your despair, give up, or get out? Only you can answer these questions. If the relationship is worth saving, then slug it out with your partner. Scratch and claw until your despair is nothing but a memory. However, if you feel the relationship contributes to the main cause of your despair then you need to reassess the relationship.

You do exist, so does your very own pain and your existence shouldn't be taken for granted.

HERE ARE A FEW THOUGHTS TO OVERCOME DESPAIR:

1. Inform your parents about your concerns or in any other situation speak to a family member. An older brother, sister, or someone you absolutely trust and who is close to you, will do the trick. Some people have psychologists. A word or two in the right psychologist's ear might be what they need. Personally, I prefer a stranger than a relative. A stranger has nothing to lose or gain from addressing your concerns, so will give you the benefit of doubt but will always apprise you of their candid thoughts.
2. Make a note of your despairs and try to resolve them with your partner. Work on them with your other half. Do always check your attitude, your anger, character and forbearance when dealing with others. Yes, you are faltering in your endeavours but with a lot of patience, an inventory of your worries and daily attitude check, you just might overcome your despair.
3. Stop blaming your partner. The patterns of despair sometimes are mutually maintained by your sly and subtle actions. Learn and try to reflect your part in the dynamic, rather than focusing on your partner's problem. It takes an act of will and recognition to reach a resolution to your despair and further a committed attachment.

RECOMMENDATION 4

YOUR RELATIONSHIP

*"Every relationship has its complications but
who cares. Yours is your only priority"*

I guess the first thing you need to determine if you are one part of a couple, is how would you define your relationship? Do not lie. Most people lie about their relationship, but please do not lie to yourself.

This is what most people say, "Yeah, it's all good". Yeah right! It is all they could ever have hope for. But how would they define it? Do not just claim your bond is perfect because of identity and a desire to conform to the norm.

Do not be deceived by your attitude. We do not exactly know how we can define our relationship, but we can do our best to summarise it truthfully. I know what you are thinking. The wonderful thing about you being in a relationship is that you are in a relationship. How wonderful, congratulations, go right ahead and chuck this book. You will be the first Romeo and Juliet couple in 400 years.

In all truth, would you consider it just right for you? Alternatively, would you deem it as better than you deserve or worse than you expected? Think about it. When you both first became acquainted, you both normally were similar in character and enjoyed pleasurable times together. You liked going to museums, art shows, or animal sacrifice, burglarising or eat dunkin' donuts on park benches, racing cars in rain, self-mutilation and so on and so forth. In the beginning, you made compromises, all the same, in the long-run you want to spend time doing those things that interest you more than those that interest your partner.

Consider those pros and cons and then answer the question. How do you define your relationship?

Just being flexible, understanding, and accepting isn't all your relationship should be. Your relationship should give you, not only a sense of belonging but also an appreciation of being loved and needed. When you are in a relationship on the verge of marriage, you are supposed to both burn for each other.

If your life were not terribly exciting, it would be worth exploring what other changes you could make before committing or breaking up with a partner. It would be worth giving yourself a deadline and fess up.

Some partners consider having sexual relationship outside of their exclusivity is harmless. If one of you prefer getting sloppy drunk, making out in cars with strangers, eating weird foods, yodelling in public or having adventures far away from the four walls of your bedroom then … hmmm …

Our purpose in having a relationship that we hope progresses to marriage is to remember flirtation and eventually having sex outside our dating parameters is sometimes adventurous but most times wide of the mark.

Most couples must engage in new and exciting things to make the health and happiness of their paring spike. The relationship will regress to normal at any point in time but that is not a warning of a doomed relationship. It just means you are human and humans cannot be merry all the time.

Relationships are hard to go through and even harder to maintain. There are compromises and heartache. If there is an equal amount of compromises between partners then they have a good partnership. I would define a good relationship is where you will be able to take to your partner without the fear of anything. One where, if you have an argument you'll be able to see their point of view or forgive their trespasses after a decent amount of time, no matter what. Say three hours. I suggest that time limits be given for all arguments, regardless of seriousness.

Bear in mind, out of a chaotic circumstance, perhaps a playground of unruly kids, a traffic accident, and a volcanic eruption, there comes the calm. Togetherness follows the simple joy of tranquillity.

TYPES OF RELATIONSHIPS

There are several types of romantic relationships, one to fit every given couple at one stage of development or another. Given our own personal history, we all have some kind of idea how *"Good"* or *"Exact"* a relationship ought to be. We needlessly distress ourselves comparing our relationships With the ideals of what truly a relationship should be like. Concluding with the self-realisation that ours is defective in comparison with others, not realising that we can open diverse doors to a broader spectrum of living productively with ourselves.

Below are a Number of Types of Relationships

Unrequited Love

At any one point in your life, you will develop an intimate, emotional connection with a man or woman who may already be in a committed relationship, or possibly, when you yourself are in a committed relationship. Nonetheless, this divine individual you adulate hardly notices your existence. Normally, this deals with first loves. Nothing physical may ever happen, but the secret yearning for this person, is unnoticeable and makes you apprehensive just even thinking about him or her. Be careful, craving, jealousy, envy, and anger go hand in hand with such one-sided love. A burning love-ache that is rarely sated.

The Long distance Kind

This is the type of relationship you tell yourself is the one to invest your efforts in. You will love to visit him or her and on every occasion, it will feel like a mini-vacation. However in due course, you will realize you want to move on. On the other hand, you do not really want to be with him or her. Alternatively, perhaps you get fed up with the relationship. Maybe because, airport lounges does not do it any more, or the thrill is gone or he or she does not want to accommodate coming to you for a change. Perhaps flights are getting expensive and you are just plain tired of it all.

Conveniency Sake.

You will date someone because he or she looks good on paper. Alternatively, for no other reason other than you should. Why? Because everybody, your friends, your family, complete strangers tell you this chick or guy is perfect, that you look good together. He or she is handsome or beautiful, they've got a great job, they have a great sense of humour, they are kind, They are totally matrimonial material and they treat you the way you deserve. But, hey hold on, the umph factor is missing. He or she does not excite you. You can have great conversations, but that inexplicable connection between you, just is not happening.

The Prizey Possessive Sort

Most influential men know the advantage of have a female bombshell on his arm. So do some rich careless but influential women whom see it as a distinction to have a handsome virile knick-knack hanging onto every wish and action of hers. Rich and insanely influential men or women are intrigued by what life is like with a particular woman or man on their arm. Gold diggers seem cheerful with a certain filthy sugar daddy, or that giddy female friend of yours who is always with a male model or athlete. Emotionally low esteemed and self-interested people typically cannot carry this type of relationship for long. As time goes by, they will have the need to crave a real honest to goodness relationship connection.

A Purely Carnal One

There may come a time when you will just have need for a purely sexual relationship. A "booty call" one, if you prefer. A relationship when you call or text one another for the sole reason to spend time together almost immediately. The bedroom is where you spend most of your time together. It is just great sexual chemistry, and for the immediate future for some reason, you never feel more compelled to explore your sexual delight in any other area.

A Fundamentally Pals Type

Everything is great except one thing: you and he or she do not feel like having sex with one another. It feels like kissing your cousin or perhaps that unattainable personality you cherish. You can have a fun day, connect on many levels, but when it comes to the bedroom, your blood runs either on the cold side or on the hot. This is a Friend with Benefit package. In rare instances, it is a joyful relationship. On the flip side, it could ruin a friendship if things went too far.

Transient

You enjoy how he or she makes you feel. There does not seem to be anything wrong with the guy or chick. You enjoy the sex and spending time with them. Yes. It's fun for all the right reason, at least for the moment. However, you wouldn't want to make plans for the future. That real zing, that va va voom ... just is not there. But, hey for the moment it is an easy, good, fulfilling distraction.

The Habituated Kind

Yes, your previous relationships were exhausting than you ever thought possible. You are emotionally, mentally, and physically drained from such a toxic relationship, despite having an extreme attraction to your partner. In any case, having such drastically diverse principles, sentiments, or integrity all you do is argue, fight and have great make up sex. You both bring out the worst in each other, but for all your intentions you cannot just stay away from each other. You are always going to be on the edge in this kind of relationship. It is like being addicted. The highs are very high and soothing, but the lows leave you debilitated and weary.

The Performing Type

Who can blame you for your actions? You need love, you really really have to want love. So you meet someone who really wants love, and so you are very willing to make many changes to accommodate it. You get a makeover and change the way your look, talk, think and socialize for her or him. He or she probably does the same for you. You actually have zero interest in each other's passions or hobbies, but you attend all related event and feign interest just like a good partner does. You appear happy to everyone except you, but in fact, it is all an act. You are not satisfying your needs, aside from the fact that you do not want to be alone. It is actually the most exhausting relationship you will have ever been in.

The Amicable Kind

We all get a little new agey at some point and tell ourselves to give this relationship a try. You are emotionally committed to one another, but are both free to have other relations with other people. This relationship only works if both parties are not that emotionally invested in one another and for this reason, it usually ends anyways.

The Rebound Sort

You, and possibly your ex have just gone through breakups and gone your separate ways. All the same, you need to feel the love you had to cover up the longing pain within, hence you begin a new one. An approximate one you once had. Well, let me tell you, this relationship almost never works out. It is fabricated from the fear of facing reality. It might be enjoyable for a while but it is ever so fragile.

The Domineering Kind

At one point, unfortunately, you might date someone who prefers to control you. They tend to set the rules for the relationship, and you will undoubtedly follow them. There is just something about him or her that makes you faint-hearted. You do not see how preposterous their directives are. Rules like not visiting your friends with or without him or her, or that you abstain from talking to not only your male friends, any male. Alternatively, that dishes should be set in the right places or stored in the right kitchen cabinet. It would be as if you are under a spell, which would be clear for anyone to see except, you. Beware this relationship and if able, avoid at all cost, unless you prefer this kind of subjugated relationship. Bear in mind, abuse does not always start with violence.

The Impartial Type

Great! You are the "IT" couple, the "Power Couple" or at least, you think you are. Everyone tells you that. What you really are is two people who do not know how or are not willing to compromise and sacrifice the image of your relationship. You always put yourself ahead of your partner, and visa versa. You are both highly focused on your careers, or your own separate social lives. Essentially you just meet up for convenient's sake. Love is definitely not a priority in this sort of relationship.

The Inter-Reliant Type

How inconvenient! You or your partner (or both of you) cannot function without the other person. You are apprehensive and despondent when you are not around one another. Areas of your life suffer as a result of it. You will often go out of your way to keep this person's love. Like give up a great opportunity to be in the vicinity with them.

IS HE OR SHE THE RIGHT PERSON FOR YOU?

How can you know if you are marrying the right person? Well, you may never truly know but there are some guidelines that can aid you in your choice;

- If you feel the kind of support and encouragement you expect from your own emotional and intellectual growth then the right person is definitely in your wheelhouse. He or she will be the one helping you stand on your own feet. Making you feel worthy, fulfilled and secure. They support in the development of your sense of purpose and the satisfaction with being yourself.

- Your right person should not be egotistical, critical, disconcerting, a slob, or a jerk. He or she will be considerate and courteous to your needs when it comes to sex and affection. They will back up the declaration "I LOVE YOU" with loving actions. Like wanting to spend time with you, noticing you are dog-gone tired, being patient and listening to you. Showing affection not only when necessary and remembering your birthdays and significant anniversaries without prompt from you. Sometimes, it is the little things that count.

- The right somebody ought to be first and foremost, an acquaintance. He or she will love the time spent with you. Both of you will be sexually compatible with each other. If not, then you had better address the problem before the wedding bells or the relationship will suffer.

- Your chosen mate should be well mannered, thoughtful, and gracious. They should be willing to make a fool of themselves, do the little courteous things, such as saying "Thank You", holding a door open and getting up from that seat for an elderly person. She would be able respect you through thick and thin, never embarrass you, fart in your presence, and not claim that it was just the salad or some shit excuse like that. Yes, this may all seem antediluvian and archaic, but it does reflect the amount of consideration and kind-heartedness in a person. On the other hand, if you prefer your preferred mate to have a little grit or is a burly biker then he or she should be open to your specific needs.

- The right spouse had better have similar goals and values to yours. Opposites attract, yes. As long as you, both agree to disagree, some of the time. All relationships need a balance of emotions, proficiencies, and vigour. You cannot have an emotional bully in a relationship with a meek sing-along type otherwise, the spark that set off that relationship will fizzle away.

- Conversations and communication should be stimulating and not dreary. They should be able to communicate thoughts and feelings that you will be able to understand without being spoken aloud.

- The only constant thing in life is change, so understanding between both of you should be a willing endeavour. Even with the right mate, you will face difficulties and differences that are contrary to your own well-being. Do not fret, after all compromise is the key to a healthy lifestyle both prior and after the wedding vows. Your chosen spouse will be willingly to encourage you to balance your work and personal life in the right degree. It is no picnic to find out you and you alone will be the only one in the relationship willing to pick up the slack.

- Finding the right person does not mean that the two of you won't have difficulties or differences to deal with. All the same, with the right person you will know that the two of you will be able to work through the issues that could hurt your relationship. You should also believe that your partner would seek professional help if you both were unable to work things through.

- Trust is the basis of any worthwhile relationship. If you cannot trust your significant other then there is no need to carry on the charade of going through an engagement. Your chosen partner should not be monitoring your movements or get jealous if you smile at the milkman or insist on seeking his or her approval before you go out or doing something you feel or want to have to do. You are your own person, control should not be a factor in a loving relationship. Rather the contrary, him, or her would want to share your experiences whenever able.

We are all born with an innate sense of good judgment or perception. An awareness that followed us from the jungle when predators were lurking nearby. I call it the *"Tracer Sense"*. These senses are heightened when there are problematic issues in your relationship. Do not ignore them or hoodwink yourself into thinking that "this too will pass" or it just "isn't important". Ignore it and possibly, without you being aware your other half will change. No. You need to face them head on, if you do not wish to carry these issues over into your hopefully jolly jovial married life.

GIRLS HERE ARE SOME SIMPLE TRUTHS TO KNOW ABOUT GUYS:

RESPECT: Men need to know that their partners respect them both privately and publicly. They thrive when they are showered with a modicum of respect, admiration, and belief from their partners. The sense of being unloved is less worse than being disrespected by their other half.

TEMPTATION: Men struggle every day with temptation. Enticement of the ophthalmic or licentious kind. Your man is bombarded with women every day, be she beautiful to him or not. This does not mean he has a wandering eye, it just means he is human and a man. He cannot avoid spotting a woman who walks a certain way, smiles with her eyes in a certain way or giggles in that manner he likes. Even if he glances at that woman, the image is stored away in that part of his cerebellum that will rematerialize whenever he looks at you. Do not fear about those glances. Men can't control these looks but they can choose to dismiss or dwell on those glances. Men have the tendencies to write simply and truthfully, when it comes to their fantasies and not their partner, which is far from being metrosexually ideal.

ROMANCE: Men, like women enjoy romance but can barely produce it. Most men appear to be prosaic globs, it does not mean they intend to be. Truthfully though, given the choice, men will take a pub over a park any day. Men want to be romantic, but they just are not wired to be that way. They tend to scatter rose petals with enough thorns to ensure they get under the skin of the most modernistic spouse. This is not to say that Men cannot be romantic, they just cannot ... exactly pull it off. They are inundated by internal qualms and possible peer pressure. A man can do better if they were encouraged by a partner who could redefine his imagination.

APPEARANCE: Your appearance is very particular to your partner. He wants you to look like that supermodel he saw in that magazine or the girl next door he admired since he was a young kid. They want their partners to make an effort to look their best even if their best is not good enough. Men appreciate the attempts or pains their girlfriends or wives make to maintain their desirability. Be conscious of the fact, that men do not need a lover who is so darn good-looking they can't see him or themselves.

SEX: Oomph! Sex is a major confidence builder in men. In contrast, surprisingly it is not because they desire it more. It is because they have a strong need to fulfil their significant other and be needed by them. The more sex, the more his sense of well-being carries over to his routine daily life. There is a downside, the less sex, or rejection from his partner, may it be for physical or emotional reasons, then he would feel a profound sense of rejection. He would no longer feel like the alpha male in his little unit but a spectator. Bottom line, men have a critical need to have that feeling of love and desire.

ANGER: When a man becomes angry with his mate, his response can be damning in various ways. Men dislike being disrespected or humiliated by their significant other, even if there is a good reason. Men thrive when they know their partner trust, admire and believe in them. If they lose or dissolve that trust, it can very soon develop into an anger that may lead to a detrimental outcome. Like living in an alcohol fuel rage or a drug dazed numbness.

INSECURITY: Most men have egos the size of the moon, some have balls the size of coconuts. You never know until you meet them.

GUYS HERE ARE SOME SIMPLE THINGS TO KNOW ABOUT CHICKS:

Never confuse intimacy with intensity. Feelings usually have the dubious fact of being good liars to us. Especially intense ones. As compelling as they are, they are not good prognosticators of our true and enduring intentions. Strangely though, they are some good certainties in them.

HOLDING HANDS: There is a custom in South America where the woman walks ahead of her spouse, showing all parties that the man behind her is hers and hers only, and if you want to approach him for whatever amenities, you would have to seek her permission first. In most ways, the holding of hands is a similar customary convention. Women like holding hands, particularly in the public domain. They cherish the thought that their partner wants to be the only hand he gets to hold. It signifies that he is hers and hers only. And not only that, it indicates that he is also full of pride to be with her.

GIFTS: Girls like little innocuous surprises. The little note he leaves before he goes to work remarking how beautiful she looked sleeping especially after the night they had. The housework chores he does before joining his mates down at the pub. Little surprises that informs her that you are thinking of her.

Here are some suggestions of the great little gifts to remember.

a) A letter tucked in her work clothes apologising for any of your actions that might have hurt her.
b) A hand written poem expressing your love to her.
c) A post-it note in her pocket letting her know you're thinking of her
d) A gift from childhood she always wanted but couldn't get herself
e) Spending a whole day with her instead of an hour or two
f) Spend time with her when she least expects it.

g) Of Course, the little inconsequential gifts do wonders too. i.e. A Picture Frame, An Adorable love Journal or A Thoughtful Throw pillow.

SEX: Ah ha! Sex is a major issue when it comes to women. Surprisingly, it is not because they crave it more. No, they need to know their man can carry his weight. Some women have little time for laziness, boredom, exhaustion or your disparate sex drive. Learn her tempo because when she is good to go so must you. Otherwise, she would lose respect for her lover and no longer feel like they would be anything but a spectator in their sexual dealings. *Sine qua non*, women also have a critical need to fulfil that *"bump an' grind"* sensation of sex and longing.

SECURITY: Girls need to know that her partner can protect her. It signifies that they care for her. Care for her, not to the point of domineering over her waking moments. That I believe is akin to stalking or abuse, depending on the rapport.

UNDERSTANDING HER: If you take the time to not only learn her likes and dislikes, but her little idiosyncrasies, it means that you are not only interested in knowing her better but you intend to find ways to make her happy.

ROMANCE: Women love romance, they go gaga for it and expect it from their partners. They love guys who can produce it at some level. If you kiss her in the rain, in the middle of traffic or when she is among friends, then you have just past a beta test for being romantic. Men do not have to be prosaic lumps when it comes to romance. A Rose at the right time in the right place could do wonders. That includes not forgetting the day you met, your anniversaries and birthdays. Women want to believe that the chase for their affections is ongoing. Men have to be romantic for their sake even if they are not wired that way. Women want men to be constant romantic gardeners for their affection and even if they cannot pull it off, the attempt more than the act itself is enough to melt a woman's heart.

APPEARANCE: She takes care of her appearance and is very particular when she is with you. She expects you to be equally careful about your appearance. She expects you to have the appearance of someone that resembles the groom on-top of a wedding cake or Brad Pitt, Denzel Washington or Robert Pattinson. That handsome actor or model she has admired since he was a young lass. She wants her partner to at least make an effort to look their best, even if their best is not actually good enough. She appreciates the attempts made to maintain their desirability.

RECOMMENDATION 5

YOUR ... "IT'S COMPLICATED"

"There are complications all the time in relationships between a man and a woman. It will be so until the end of time"

Relationships do not come in black and white fact-check lists or with an instruction manual. There are so many shades of grey within our interactive restrictions that we never know whether we are coming or going.

Yes, each situation is complicated, especially yours. No one sees it but you. Why else would you consider your relationship status as "Its Complicated". Don't feel lost. You are not the only one dealing with complications in your love life. Relationships at all times can be tricky to explain and a complication that defines your situation is noteworthy.

Complications on your path or in a relationship can arise for several reasons. From falling in and out of love, to a bitter remark, or a confusion of financial affairs or a past life, you would prefer dead and buried.

Except for the complications in your life, your wife-to-be or future husband should be the most important person. Scores of issues can define your situation. Children, illness, pets, socialising, wealth or therein lack of, emotional baggage, family or job. It is best you do not try to solve the complication alone.

Saying "It's complicated" can mean anything.

Here are some examples of the complicated hurdles you might face:

I. **GUILT**: One partner in the relationship wants out while the other cannot do without the other. The partner that wants to let go feels the guilt of not getting the best out of the relationship and wants to let go. He or she ought to do what's best for himself or herself. Sometimes this can be harrowing experience that might lead to stalking and violent, unnecessary actions.

II. **TRUST**: Trust is the key to any relationship. There will be times when you might notice certain things or you might have unresolved issues preventing you from trusting each other. You have to be realistic. Ask the question directly of what is bothering you and try to let things go. It will surely make you enjoy each other more. You have to learn to be fair in any argument, be sensitive to each other feelings, listen to her or his side of the story, do your fair share of workload, forgive, and do not overreact. You both have issues and feelings, so being consistent and doing what you promised to each other is a sure way to respect each other's boundaries.

III. **FAMILY**: There is always an unknown quantity when it comes to family. I would not even pretend what that dynamic is, none of us do. Some say family is all you can trust. In reality, if that were true, then the world would be a very small place to live in. There are always complications with family. At times, it is just better to believe in yourself and damn the family.

IV. **ADDICTION**: A major complication in marriages is alcoholism and drug addiction. These impediments do not help any situation, not to mention marriage. It is a complication that may be on going or unmanageable.

V. **An On and Off Relationship**: Is this really a on and off relationship or a Love Triangle? The novelty of the on and off courtship has worn off or your lover may insist you make a choice. What do you do? The easiest way is by having an honest conversation with your partner. Even if by speaking with them, you risk losing a relationship even ending one altogether. Your partner maybe furious about the relationship but you no longer have to live in denial or avoid confronting the situation.

VI. **FRIENDS WITH BENEFIT**: Most people are sceptical of "Fuck Buddies". An association devoid of emotion but of compulsive sex. I mean, how could you fuck your friend again and again without having some sort of stable relationship or falling in love? A carnal aspect with no illusions about being dynamic. Agreed, having a friend with benefits is less aggravating, it is more of a low-intensity familiarity unencumbered by responsibilities. You get all the groovy accouterments about being in a quasi-relationship, fantastic sex, snuggles (if so inclined), their secrets, minus the baggage and messy commitment aggravations that go hand in hand with a habitually styled relationship.

A "FWB" bond can sometimes lead to hedonism and the sexual discovery of one or both partners. This will of course lead to an equally high concentration of bitterness. Why? Because despite ourselves, we are all innately selfish and live in a Fountainhead centered world, whether we like it or not. There are perhaps only two advantages in benefiting from a fuck buddy and that is it promotes an open bubble of transparency and is a great exercise in non-possessiveness.

VII. **CHILDREN**: Children are sticky, noisy, and smelly. Pooh! And do you know what is in their diapers? Jeeze. Nevertheless, children are the joy of a couple's life. If its kids that define your circumstances then you will know outright that, children will undoubtedly set the mood for your relationship and your future happiness. Up front, you should be aware that even with the best of marriages, dealing with children will be challenging and more often than not you will feel confined, out of control and even powerless. If you do not want kids or have children or just one kid, your situation will be blatantly obvious to your proposed partner. The woman would be looking for a father or at least a father-like-figure to dote on her kids. The man would be seeking a mother to comfort or soothe his kids in a way only a woman can. If you are comfortable with his or her kids then go for it, provided the children are comfortable with you. Off hand though, most relationships suffer a gradual increase in conflicts whenever children are involved. Even if there is a cumulative erosion of satisfaction over time, parents do experience less depression or stress as children grow over time. That is not to say it is a major boon to separations or divorces.

Children instinctively sense when their parents are upset or in conflict, even if they do not show it. They feel obligated to absorb the emotional needs of their parents leaving them depressed and stressed. Especially, if a parent calls on them to take sides in a parental dispute. This kind of situation should be avoided at all times, because tensions can build into a pressure of the powder-keg variety. Thankfully, children can be resilient creatures and either tend to shove the effects of their parents' anxieties to the back of their mind or act upon it.

Unfortunately, when homely pressure does tend to be released, it reacts in various, unpredictable and sometimes combustible ways.

The solution to matrimonial happiness where children are involved will depend on the decision-making processes both partners put in place, like the division of labour, monetary problems and the general use of their time. Their disputes and differences of opinions will have to be negotiated to sustain the cooperation and respect they have for each other. It will be important to take timeout's whenever their quarrels involve a kid or kids.

Of course, the situation will be drastically different if either partner does not have the capacity to produce kids.

VIII. **SEPARATION**: Legally married for years but living alone and living the life of a single person. This is not ideal for most people especially if they have not made any steps towards separating legally. In common law marriages this might be ok but still.

IX. **COMMUNICATION**: We are fortunate that in today's society, there are several methods on how engaged couples can communicate and share their feelings. Regrettably, communication does not necessarily mean sharing. Finding ways to communicate openly about challenges is the first step toward an effective relationship. Most problems arise when couples cannot only identify their problems, they do not know to express their preferences, unless they have frank open interactions. With no communications, there are no discussions. No discussions, no solutions. No solutions result in feelings of distance and lack of intimacy. Thankfully, social media texting is a good way to start. Yes, Love hurts but you can certainly deal with it.

Here are three rules when it comes to communicating via texting.

Before the "I Dos" & Other Compendiums

a) Do not be too pushy or be so misogynistic. Reply simple texts. It will control the conversation and situation up to a point and in-effect your feelings.
b) Create internally and copy poste-haste.
c) Forget the dating rules or whatever rules you think are appropriate. You are having complication problems. What you text must be meaningful to your situation.

X. **HEALTH**: One of life's little quandaries is having to go to a dark place and deal with the pain of human frailty. This sometimes manifests itself in accidents or chronic illnesses. Some people dwell on it and carry it like a chastity belt round their shoulders, others romanticise it, while most forward thinking people accept it and move on. Experiences of this nature do put a damper on a healthy wedded life, but when you love someone enough to exchange places with them, then it shouldn't be an obstacle rather it should be defining moment. Anyone acquainted with this, could also be conversant with loss. If he or she does remember the experience but does not harp or fret about it, knows that to affect the greater good and learn from it, one has to have perspective. With perseverance and steadfastness, there are numerous ways to deal with the everyday strain of a chronic illness and your relationship. If its illness, then you will have to seek within yourself on how to go about resolving your feelings and anxieties, knowing that, eventually your partner may not always be by your side.

Learn to gain some measure of control by considering speaking to doctors knowledgeable in the specific illness. On the other hand, consider counselling. A therapist, priest, or some other trained professional. Your choice.

Distance yourself but watch out for depression, clinical or otherwise. Next to Cancer, Depression is the silent killer.

XI. **MONETARY CONCERNS**: It is a sad truth that money plays the highest of our significant priorities when it comes to choosing a mate. Either he has plenty of it or she has. Perhaps they are both paupers, it does not matter.
Even before the wedding is over money plays a predominate problem.

Here are some complicated financial issues that have to addressed before the wedding bells ring.

a) Is there going to be a household account? What percentage of your salaries are you both contributing to maintain the home? Is it going to be weekly or monthly income household?

b) Don't blame one another for any financial woes that maybe approaching

c) Do you want your partner to know how much income you earn, monthly or annually?

d) Set aside a convenient time to discuss the subject of your financial situation. Do not broach the issue in the heat of an argument.

e) How well-off are either of you?

f) Have you both resolved the mortgage problem? Are you getting one and how much have you settled on?

g) What will both your workweek be like and how much are you allowed to spend within those hours?

h) Create a joint budget proposal including all finances as well as savings. A scheme that you both will adhere to.

i) How ambitious are you both? Are you both contented with the other's level of ambition.

j) Which of you is responsible for keeping the house, garden and allotment cared for and organised? How much are you both contributing for their upkeep?

k) How financially secure are you both should the unexpected should happen?

I) Make a decision as a couple concerning your immediate and long-standing financial aspirations. You may include your individual goals too, but set aside some appropriate monetary plans for your parent's financial needs as their age will in due course catch up to them.

XII. **GETTING BACK TOGETHER**: Sometimes, it is easier to end a relationship than patching things up, especially if there are way too many impediments are involved. However, if the relationship is worth saving and you really love your partner it is suggested you take a chance, for the moment. Such a relationship almost never works out, especially if you are stuck out at the painful end of the relationship. Like may be you are being used or your partner is the selfish type. Walk out of the relationship and don't turn back if you cannot work out your differences. It will hurt, but tough it out, because when one door closes, another one surely opens..

XIII. **YOUR IDOL**: Then there is the "Hero fixation" that some of us tend to drift to. It is not only complicated, it's trouble, with a capital "T". Don't mistake me, there is something cathartic about being a partner to someone who is a superhero. Unfortunately, not only does the world teach us that such a relationship is temperamental at best. Consider this, does Superman really need Lois Lane or does Lois Lane need Superman? Tell me, do you really need a hero? Do you need someone whom you look to for an escape to any particular impediment? Or is it possible you are looking for salvation. Being someone's Sgt Rock, John Connor, James Bond, in short a knight in shining armour, will eventually teach you the value of coming second in the relationship. In short, discontent. Having someone play the role of your personal saviour may be great and maybe your true path to great happiness but it is also is a recipe for disaster. Please do not get me wrong, doing things, even the little things for a loved one is great. You tend to receive and give off intense feelings. It not only makes you feel good you gain a huge dose of affection. But hey, wait. What kind of life would you have? Imagine for a moment being in Love with someone you look up to like say … Che Guevara or Donald Trump. Someone you would have sex with at any time. Would it feel or be like love? What if your hero doesn't exactly meet up with your expectations? You know that adage "Never meet your hero". Well the same applies here. "Never have sex with your hero". How complicated would that be?

XIV. **LONG-DISTANCE RELATIONSHIPS**: By definition, a long distant relation is complicated at all times. They are hard to maintain and take a toll on any relationship. Emotions are stretched and longings are varied.

Nonetheless, here are some ideas on how to manage those long distance yearnings.

a) It can be a good idea to send photo texts activities of your day or week.
b) It could be a wonderful idea to send good morning text messages and having goodnight conversational calls.
c) Never get distracted on those long or short phone calls you rarely share.
d) Send him or her surprise care packages to let them know you are thinking of them.
e) Surprise visits are rarely welcomed but at times, it is best you do surprise him/her with a visit. However, do try to plan for some visits and of course date night activities.
f) Have fun on your visits and make sure to laugh together.

XV. **SOCIALISING**: The old school method of a good friend hooking you up with a friend or introducing you or that cute meet when you just bump into your soulmate are not so over as you might think. It's still the tried and true method for socialising. On the flip side, dating in today's social media world requires dating apps and numerous application feelers. If your complicated problem is due to your inability to socialise then you are not the only one. Attracting the opposite sex or even a partner in the same dominion is hard for many people. It cannot be helped. Stop worrying about the pressures of having a partner, learn first the act of socialising and things just might fall into place. If you can mould your personal interests into sociable spheres, like joining a writer's arena, a sci-fi club, taking up sky-diving, bungee jumping or aerial yoga, whatever your interests, you will be able to build your social influences. I know it is not easy, but do not worry, in most extreme form, kindred souls tend to gravitate to each other. Extroverts tend to bump and grind to the beat of any music. Baby steps are the way to go. It may force you out of your comfort zone and the more you get involved, the better for your social standing. Your personal strength, attractive qualities, and confidence will increase. Getting out of your comfort zone, not just physically but mentally. It will surely pull you out of a downward or dead end spiral. Think of the undertakings you could get involved with and overcome, as bus stops towards the journey of love. However, under no circumstance do you join these clubs or partake in these quests with sole purpose of attracting a partner. You will find it unproductive and futile. Be natural and let your partner seek you out. It is my bet she or he will find you more enduring if he or she finds that you appreciate him or her for who they are.

XVI. **NEW "UNDETERMINED" RELATIONSHIP**: You have a new person in your life, you are having a great time and yet when asked what he or she is to you, you promptly reply, "Just a friend". You have been seeing each other for a while and have not put a label on the relationship. Yes, we know you are having fun, a great time in this relationship. It is new, fresh and exciting, and not having a name to it is the best part. Hurrah for you. It is best you put a name to that as quickly as possible.

These days it is not so necessarily complicated to have an exclusive relationship. Especially, when the more permissible and accepting societies still regard the status norm as monogamy. To most of us, it is still the more desirable and customary way to engage a relationship.

Most of us do not want more emotional crisis than the ones we already have. It will be like carrying two times your weight while standing on a tightrope. That goes for potential life partners too.

No one wants that partner with irrational ex'es, bastard children tugging at their skirt or trousers, acrimonious family stories or scarring childhood memories.

No complication in a relationship is ever alike. Ironing out the complication in your own way may be your best bet to solve your impediment.

Never believe that shortcuts like marriage, or having a baby is the solution to any complicated relationship problem. It is not. Relationships get harder, not easier, after we marry and move along the life cycle. Do not believe in the power of your love or nagging to create something later that is not there right now or ever has been. Believe that sometime in the near future your complication will be but a memory.

RECOMMENDATION 6

DO YOU REALLY WANT TO MARRY ME?

"Love is an ideal thing, marriage a real thing"

We never understand the good side of a marriage or whether we are ready for one just yet, until that marriage itch beckons. If you are not ready for marriage, it is because you are not certain the right partner is beside you or you have doubts about him or her. Alternatively, maybe because you do not have a secure job, or your life is not at all it should be. Or perhaps for a million different special reasons.

Giving a serious thought with an open mind will provide an understating to just how meaningful and satisfying a delightful contented marriage can be. A happy marriage can change a couple's life for the better.

Having said that, more often than not, there are unknown and discerned reasons that make up all the major and good excuses to avoid marriage.

HERE ARE SOME REASONS TO GET MARRIED:

COMMITMENT:

Can you put a name to your relationship? Have you been dating for years? You will have to define it somehow. A dating relationship is considered too casual to be a marriage and if you really care for your partner, why wouldn't you want it to proceed to the next step? Marriage will be the ethical bond that will define your relationship with your partner as more than just a casual fling. However, the minute you do not see your relationship as a casual thing anymore or marriage as a lock without a key, it will be an affirmation that you are ready for the highest commitment. Only then can you give to the one you love the proof of your love for them.

PEER PRESSURE:

Society has a way of criticizing couples if they are not fulfilling their duties as a unified couple, hence peer pressure. When it comes to getting married, peer pressure is an important tradition. Tradition is tradition, and it does not stop, even after the vows have been exchanged. Wives feel the pressure to keep a clean, healthy home for her partner and their children. Men are required to provide security, be the breadwinner and produce children. All the while, both partners have to answer to their family and friends. Yes, there is a lot of peer pressure for both partners. The most pressure will stem from family members who do not approve of the spouse their daughter or son has chosen. For example, if a married couple gets into a fight while their parents or friends are present they will undoubtedly feel the pressure for them to pick a side and vice versa. On the whole, peer pressure can help or destroy a family.

SHARING YOUR LIFE:

Life is a game of phases, from our teen years to our single years. We party, share our laughs, have our one nightstands, meaningless flings all leading to marriage. Marriage is a pretty important phase in life. It is a whole experience that is worth the ride, until you grow tired of it. Evolving from being a social creature, to one that needs or requires the attention of a partner is a normal development. It means you feel the need to be watched over by someone who will be able to share the happy and sad moments in your life.

Having someone who is willing to grow old with you, sees life through your eyes and whom you can call your own, will feel more meaningful, important and fulfilling. Just knowing you have someone, understands your preferences and your principles and vice versa will feel more satisfying and provide meaning to your existence.

TRADITION:

Tradition is tradition, and part a big part of tradition is getting married. Marriage that stand's the test of time is also a tradition. It is the norm but not always the exception. It is the written and an even unwritten archaic law in most well meaningful society that getting married to the one you love and who loves you is the right, lawful and respectable way to live with each other.

IN LOVE:

The minute you admit you are in love, and you have confirmation that your feelings are reciprocated, then the easier things will slot into place. Does he or she make you feel alive and happy? Do they make you smile, can they carry a conversation, is worthy of you and wants to spend the rest of his or her life with you? If the answer is yes, then perhaps you have found your soulmate. What better way to commit than getting married.

SUPPORT SYSTEM:

The best support system in life is being married. Financially and emotionally both of you can lead your lives and aspirations with each other in mind. You both will lend each other the strength and determination you need to pursue your goals and ambitions with renewed vigor. Whenever you are in the throes of a challenging conundrum, just realizing you have a partner who can share and ease your burden can assist you towards a better viewpoint or outlook.

RESPONSIBILITY:

With marriage comes a greater maturity and responsibility in life. Some shy away from that, especially men. However, once there is love a marriage can build trust, faith and commitment. It makes a boy grow into a man, making him more responsible for himself and his spouse. It also makes a girl become a woman, giving her the emotional security of a stable relationship

PROCREATION:

Most commercials on TV show a loving couple with that adorable 2.4 family unit enjoying a park. Playing, laughing, doing cute things, and basically having fun. Do not be fooled. Children take a lot of work. When you are ready to walk down that aisle, you should already have settled the debate of having children. Yes, children are a joy to behold but make certain your reasons for having them are valid ones, because affection, patience and care are the adjectives you will need for bringing up children.

ACHIEVEMENTS:

Yes, you have everything that you ever wanted. A fast car, maybe several. A beautiful home, maybe more than a few. Money, money, money and what else. These are just material possessions. Yes, they do provide a certain happiness, but do they give meaning to your life? Having someone who loves you unconditionally will always contribute more to your happiness than any material possessions that you own.

PARENTS:

You cannot help having parents. Whether they are positive influences or not. Any marriage will aid your parents in feeling more at ease about your future. They may not voice it, but getting married to the one you love is damn reassuring to both families. It will make them feel contented to know that you and your spouse have a happiness that will flourish and that you both will be there through thick and thin for each other. Oh and let us not forget the joy of playing with their grandkids.

MEANING TO LIFE:

Most marriages bring a certain focus in life. A certain responsibility not only for yourself, but also for your partner. A reliability that will create a new kind of entity that breathes life as a couple. Maybe a bigger, more prosperous job, more satisfaction and meaning to your existence.

TYPES OF MARRIAGE

MONOGAMY: is where one person marries one other person. It is the norm and most common of marriages. Of course a spouse can marry again only on the death of a previous spouse or divorce. This is called Serial Monogamy.

POLYGAMY: Is where one person marries multiple spouses at any given time. A function of looking at a marriage from a sociological viewpoint gives meaning into some marital arrangements. This a practice made popular by Mormons and African Chiefs. Polygamy is illegal in Britain and the States.

Motives for Marriage

There are several reasons that for marrying.

1. The desire to have children. Having a family is among the highest priority for many people.

2. The desire for love, perpetuity, companionship, commitment and continuity.

3. There are ephemeral reasons for marriage such as peer pressure, social legitimacy and the desire for a high social status.

4. Other motivations include economic viability, social agitation or revenge, or even the most plausible reason, the validation of an unplanned or unwanted pregnancy.

RECOMMENDATION 7

"I LOVE YOU" SHOULDN'T BE A PUNCHLINE

*"I can't say any more than I love you.
Anything else would be a waste of breath"*

Someone once asked me 'When do you know marriage is the next step?'

I answered rather acerbically, 'When you can't afford not to go through with it'

I believe in true love, the magic of love, that special person, hell I even believe in the practice of suitable arranged marriages. Yes, I do and so does 33% of the planet. That also means there is such a thing as Love at first sight and undying love.

Of course, me and thirty-three percent of the human race could be jaded to the fact that love is such a rare commodity that it doesn't exist.

Today people view the words "I love you" as an afterthought. It is not and should not ever be. These words should be sacrosanct and uttered with great care. Like it should be. Both partners, when saying these words to each other should regard the declaration as something special they both care for.

These days, the words "I love you" in addition to acts of love are being used very often in various households that the true meaning seems lost. I don't doubt that this creates a very safe, comfortable, welcoming, trusting, and non-judgmental environment but it does every now and then prove the reverse.

A friend developed her distinct definition of love through a household that conversed with different bad or worse disparities of love lingoes. From what I currently understand, Favours and Deeds of Service were the family's primary love communications.

When introduced to a different relationship environment, she had to come up with an alternative way of conversing. She had no idea of how her tryst would or should unfold and the tricky part was trying to learn and understand her partner's love language. To make matters worse she was an ordinary girl who enjoyed and depended on the regular things, a deed and benefit type relationship. In the early days, it felt like she was learning an alien tongue, it did not make any sense to her. In any case, when she realised that the love language was an annoying necessity, she finally became aware of the distinct love languages and she was much better able to understand the other dynamics concerned with the language of love.

Here are a few rules for both parties, to keep in mind involving LOVE.

1. Give only as much love, as you are willing to give yourself. Remember, People can only love you as much as you are willing to accept or give, no matter how much love they actually have for you to accept.
2. If you are feeling down, it is because you are relying on something outside of yourself to feel good, gain affirmation, or make you happy.
3. The only certainty is your own uncertainty. This can be a good thing on the other hand it maybe not.

IF HE REALLY LOVES YOU:

To settle that doubting thought in your mind, does he or does he not love you, here are some pointers that could steer you in the right direction.

1. **Bragging**: If he brags about you, then he's your biggest fan. If he brags too much, then he is your biggest fan and/or fanatic. Take care.

2. **Sacrifice:** If he makes sacrifices for you and your happy to do the same then opportunities are abound for both of you.

3. **Values:** If he shares the same values as you then you might be on the path to true happiness. You both want kids and you both expect to split the childcare equally. Or maybe you both want kids and he wants to take extended paternity leave. Maybe you've also agreed that you should each get 45 minutes to yourself to go to the gym every day, or you plan to buy a home and move to the suburbs in five years. You know you're on the same page with things that matter most to you because you've discussed them.

4. **Even after years together, he still does little chivalrous things for you.** Like open doors for you, or carry you to your doorstep when your feet hurt after wearing high heels all day and you just cannot bear to walk one more block.

5. **He doesn't try to change you.** He knows you're messier than him, that you always need a pet cat, and can't cook to save your life, and all of that is all right by him.

6. **When you think about marrying him, the best part isn't the wedding, it's the idea of spending your lives together.** The wedding is fun, but you really cannot wait

for the two weeks right after when you'll get uninterrupted honeymoon time.

7. **You survived a long-distance relationship.** It was hard and scary, but you love each other so much that you were able to make the necessary sacrifices to make it through with a singular goal in mind: living in the same place and being together when it was all over.

8. **"I miss you" isn't just a sweet thing you say:** It's a reality. Those three words are establishing and soothing verses to the ear of a loved one. Even if it hasn't been that long (like, two hours) since you saw each other.

9. **You don't like having a roommate and love having your own space, but you'd still prefer to live with him.** You look forward to the end of the day, not because you'll be done with work but because you'll get to see him again.

10. **He's your go-to person whenever you have a story to share, about work, about friends, about anything.** You used to tell your parents and friends about all these things, but now you don't call them quite as much as you used to. They don't mind because they see how happy you are.

11. **You feel comfortable planning things six months — or a year — into the future.** You're not worried you'll have to cancel plane tickets or say you won't be needing a plus-one after all. You feel that confident in your relationship.

12. **You can cry in front of him without feeling embarrassed.** He knows when to worry and when you're just caught up in a scene of a movie.

13. **When your friends complain about their significant, others or the guys they've gone out with, you get

somewhat quiet because you don't have much to contribute. You don't want to brag, but you just don't have to deal with any of that nonsense because your significant other is great to you.

14. **He's close with your family, and he's made sure you've gotten to know his.** He'll call your dad or your grandma without any hesitation. It just makes sense that you'd go to his nephew's birthday party, even if he's not there.

15. **He cares about your friends.** If one of them is having a bad day, he suggests you go spend time with her or invite her to join the two of you for dinner. If he hasn't heard someone's name in a while, he asks how she's doing.

16. **He lets you vent.** Sometimes when something frustrates you, you just need to go over it repeatedly. He doesn't get annoyed at this, and he dismisses your apologies. The only thing that bothers him about the situation is that you're upset and he wishes you weren't.

17. **He tells you, out of the blue, that you look hot.** And it's on the day you didn't dry your hair or put on makeup or even change out of your T-shirt and sweatpants.

18. **You can do things like travel together without fighting.** We've all seen (or been there) that tragic couple fighting over where to get lunch at the airport so badly that one of them devolves into tears and puts her shades on indoors and lies across three seats in the terminal. You can do tedious things with your S.O. without all the fighting.

19. **He plans activities that he knows you'll enjoy.** He doesn't depend on you to be in charge of everything, and

he remembers that you said you wanted to go to that new restaurant or museum exhibit.

20. **He works hard at his job, but you're his priority.** If you ask him to go to an event that's important to you, he's not afraid to step out of the office to accompany you. He'll figure out a way to get his work done, just as you would do for him.

IF SHE REALLY LOVES YOU:

To tell if your partner loves you, here are some pointers that could steer you in the right direction.

1. **You both have survived a long-distance relationship.** It was hard and scary, but you love each other so much that you were able to make the necessary sacrifices to make it through with a singular goal in mind: Living apart and being together when it was all over.

2. **Love your neighbour as yourself.** Good advice. Loving ourselves before we can love anyone else is a daunting task. However, if you don't express love towards yourself every now and then, you might not be able to express love to your partner. Honour yourself, your words, and your promises. If you can honour yourself and promises, I bet there will be a reward for you. Whatever the situation honour and keep yourself in mind first and hold yourself accountable if you fail. Start holding yourself accountable to yourself. No longer allow things to slide just because no one else will know. Hold yourself true to your words because they're YOUR WORDS and THEY MATTER. You're the most important person in your world, so why not build more love for yourself by keeping your words to YOU. YOU deserve it.

3. **Values:** If she shares the same values as you then you might be on the path to true happiness. You don't want kids. You both enjoy each other's company too much to allow "Rugrats" to spoil your serenity. Alternatively, maybe you both want kids and she wants to take extended maternity leave. Maybe you've also agreed that you should each get 45 minutes to yourself to go to the gym every day, or you plan to buy a home and move to the suburbs in five years. You know you're on the same page with things that matter most to you because you've discussed them.

4. **Affection, Love and Sex**: It is important that she is someone who understands your wants and is agreeable to your needs when it comes to sex and affection. "I Love You" will not be spoken but will be shown by loving actions.

5. **She doesn't like your den but appreciates you needing your own space:** You look forward to spending time with friends in your man cave. Not because you don't want to spend time with her but you need some breathing room. A place where you can unwind and be alone with your own thoughts.

6. **When you think about marrying her, the best part is the idea of spending your lives living happily ever after.** The wedding, the honeymoon was amazing, but you really can't wait to get home and begin your lives together.

7. **She doesn't try to change you.** She knows you're cleaner than she is, that you always want a pet dog, and that you need to spend a certain amount of time apart with your friends and all of that is all right by her.

8. **She's not only your friend but also your go-to person whenever you have something worrying on your**

mind. You used to tell your boys and co-workers about what is bothering you now, you don't call them quite as much as you used to. They don't mind because they see how happy you are.

9. **You can show fear in front of her without feeling ashamed.** She knows you worry and fear for both your lives together and sympathizes.

10. **Your spouse is close with your family and has made sure you have gotten to know hers or his.** They will call your mother or your parents without any hesitation. Arranges that birthday party of your niece that you have forgotten, even if they are not present.

11. **She lets you give vent to your frustrations.** When you need to vent you just need to do it. No matter who is about, she doesn't get annoyed at this and sets aside your regrets. The only thing that bothers her about the situation is that you are upset and she wishes you were not.

12. **She plans activities that she knows you'll enjoy.** She sometimes likes to be in charge of everything, and remembers what you said about that Arsenal match and those friends of yours coming over.

13. **She cares about your friends.** There is one particular friend of yours she dislikes, but for your sake, she puts up with him or her. She suggests you invite him or her to join the two of you for dinner. If she hasn't heard one of your friends name in a while, she asks how they're doing.

14. **Your Ego:** All men have humongous egos. Your ego could be the biggest blocker of love your life. Sustaining it and Keeping it in check is hard, especially when you become

reactive rather than proactive. When you're with the person you love, leave your ego behind. Your ego isn't you. It's a poor surface version of yourself. YOU deserve the true you just as much as your spouse.

15. **Trust and Honesty:** Your spouse will trust you and not monitor your text messages, computer usage or time your absence. She or he will not try to isolate you from your friends and family. He or she will have some control over your life but as much as you control hers. Your unideal partner will have you walking on eggshells half the time. You don't want that.

16. **Communication, Goals and Value.** You and your spouse will have different likes and opinions. It is only natural, just as long you agree to disagree at times. You will always argue with your chosen partner, all the same, it will not be boring but refreshingly interesting and informative every time. Your feelings and thoughts will be exchanged and the hurts and concerns will be out for discussion instead of being bottled up inside.

RECOMMENDATION 8

OUR IMPRESSIONS

"The heart of any marriage, are the memories made"

What is it that we find alluring in our partners? It begins with that first impression. For some, it is the smile of that unknown man or woman. For some it is the feet. For others, it maybe the buttocks or laugh or dimples. Whatever it is about that person, that first impression can be lasting.

Most marriages do not end up like King Seretse's and Ruth Williams or regrettably like that of Anthony and Cleopatra. Romance's that suffered from first impressions because of dubious political strife and opposition. Impressions are what we make of them. Our impressions, at times fool our senses. Beware the partner whose first impression you cherish, doesn't exactly correspond with their behaviour. A partner who is rude to waiters and travellers on the Underground or one who needs to know your every move. What you had for lunch at work? Who you met and what you talked about. A partner who would require you call or text or signify you're thinking about him or her hour by hour. A partner who would make you uncomfortable during sex or embarrass you or give no considerations to your feelings whatsoever (even if he or she rocks your world)is not one to invest your future with.

Such a partner might not manifest psychological tendencies at the present time but once things get serious then ... well take a clip from "Fatal Attraction" the movie.

IMPRESSIONS TO BE AWARE OF FOR BOTH PARTNERS

Know what you can compromise on ... and what you can't:

Maybe it's not so important that he or she likes cheese products and she talks too loud in the movies. Nevertheless, some things are deal breakers. Write your own list, if you haven't already and refer to it. It may include addictive behaviors, dishonesty, irresponsibility, defensiveness, trouble listening, immaturity, reactivity, etc.) *When it's a deal breaker get out sooner rather than later.* Ditto; if you spot a big red flag waving in your face.

Focus on your own life plan that neither requires nor excludes marriage:

Keep your primary focus on your own goals and life plan, which will put you on the firmest footing whether you marry or not. Love will either find you or hit you in the face when you least expect it. Don't forget that there are many possibilities for intimacy and connection other than pairing up.

Do not be conflict-avoidant:

This is not an invitation to engage in non-productive fighting and blaming that goes nowhere. Do not preserve the peace by silencing yourself. Enlarge and deepen the conversation when you are feeling disappointed or angry. Those are the honest emotions. You won't recognise a prospective partner (or yourself) if you don't take the conversation to the next level and test out whether this potential companion is defensive or fair-minded when you have a legitimate request or complaint.

Become an unencumbered observer:

Examine your other half with their close unit. Family and friends. It would also be prudent to observe him or her with your family and friends. At no time should you insulate the rapport and association. Observe how he or she treats their parents, the shopkeeper and the neighbor. If we were in 1984 what kind of citizen will he or she be at work and at home.

Scrutinize yourself too:

If you're too accommodating, conflict-avoidant, eager to please, either or both desperate to make it work, you won't get to know a prospective partner. Slow things down and practice having a clear, strong, assertive voice in the relationship. Use dating as an opportunity to practice having a strong voice and bringing more of your authentic self into the relationship.

Consider whether you'd want this person to be one of your best friends if you had no romantic interest:

Do not tolerate behaviors in a partner that you wouldn't settle for in a good friend. Friends sometimes have the objectivity to see the truth even if it is staring you in the face. Whether they tell you or not is another thing. Ask yourself how your friends will view the impressions you see so very treasurable in your potential partner.

RECOMMENDATION 9

WHAT'S ... LOVE?

"How on earth are you ever going to explain in terms of chemistry and physics so important a biological phenomenon as first love?" – Albert Einstein

Love is ....
Love isn't ....
Love is...
Love is not ...

Love is not an easy subject to define. Academics, singers, psychologists, actors, songwriter, poets, artists, scientists, and all those with the affinity for passion have attempted to define love or at least tried to but to no avail.

Everyone, from Shakespeare to Tennyson, your gardener, the shop clerk behind the kiosk you go to every morning, your boss, your dentist ... everyone has a different take on how they would define love. How does one define an emotion that can also be confused with infatuation and lust?

The poet's define love as *"one being aware of its existence and design, a truly biological potion brewed to perfection within our species advancement"*. According to them, it is the only time we give ourselves the permission to seek out a more significant other that could change us physically and mentally.

Ah poets. You have got to love them.

Scientists would define the notion of love as a fairy tale. The testament for scientists that people can be romantically affected by a chemical convergence of emotion would be regarded as junk science. Love to them is a condition. *"A temporary human condition that is chemically triggered by a semi-euphoric emotional reaction"*. How very quaint and technical.

Psychologists have a different take. They definitely have attempted to define love. It is just like them to complicate matters. They categorised love into three constituents. *Passion*, *Intimacy*, and *Commitment*. Those damn therapists. Here's their transcendent two-cent settee definition.

Passion is for the sexual and physical aspirations to love. Commitment being a conscious decision to "Love and Behold" come rain or shine. While Intimacy is the responsive attribute to share a connection and closeness to a particular individual.

Ha! Trust the head shrinkers to clinically pour scorn on the meaning of love. Hey, what do they know anyhow?

Well, let me give it a try.

Love is everything and not anything. Love is a severe mental disease or better still Love is a madness of the soul.

No, that doesn't do it. No that does not do it justice at all. Maybe I could do better. Love is doing stupid, bold, dangerous and magnanimous things to justify our feelings for a certain someone or one another.

No, that also doesn't do it fairness. No, I cannot define it.

Here is one definition I heard some time ago.

Love is cleaning SHIT up.

I never thought much about it until I gave it some thought.

Just imagine back to your youth when you wanted that pet gold fish, turtle, hamster, or dog and after many a tearful insistence, your parents finally succumb to your wish. I bet for the first few months you loved that pet of yours more than your parents but it meant that you literally cleaned up its shit. A friend married the woman who was willing to roll up her sleeves and work by his side as he cleaned up his shit. That can be defined as Love.

Yes, love is like cleaning up shit. It is also chaotic, byzantine, painful and most of all, a risk. More than a risk, because love lies in the heart where your experiences and the memories of your soul reside. Opening it to love is not easy. Handing it over to someone else is infinitely more difficult. It is you handing over your partner the pulse and beat of your heart and trusting them not to stop and then stomp on it.

Holy hell. What do you think?

How about this definition, Love is a selfless spiritual devotion to all life. Does it ring true? Maybe for the religious among us. Among the spiritualists, I think they would define love as the very essence to the meaning of our existence.

A friend once mentioned that Love is never having to quarrel. That to me is just crock and I wondered why she thought love is having not to argue. It was a mystery to me until I found out she had just started seeing someone and was in the throes of lust, the beginning of something new and fresh. Then it all made sense.

Okay, so you are a nice person. You do not argue with the milkman, your doctor, or that assistant of yours who never knocks on the door before she enters a room. That is not anything. At times, Love should be alive and scrappy. If you can't unburden yourself of your emotions then you should be a robot or "Spock" from Star Trek. That sort of love is like a calm pond you sit in until it becomes full and tense with a blue black bile of your waste. If there is not enough passion in your relationship to make you angry then when do you smile? You know, not a polite pleasant smile but a hurt your ears smile. Lovers need to be able to air their grievances, argue to their hearts content to clear up their differences.

In my mind, Love should be about faith. Faith in bestowing your heart to someone who will cheat, lie and betray you and you will still love him or her unconditionally. Someone you will love forever and a day. That someone whose hair will turn grey or fall off, who will grow sagging in all the wrong places and still you will love the ground they walk on.

Another definition is that love is having lots of mind-blowing sex, which is understandable. Most people these days seek love with their genitalia. Quite literally and figuratively. Giving the cover of most sensational tabloid magazines this is not surprising. They mostly advice that your spouse would care about you more if you provide him or her with mind-blowing orgasms. Men are predominately predisposed to sow their oats, while women are conditioned to respect, console and contend with the needs of men. This is quite a conundrum when it comes to any love that has to grow together.

Here is a secret. No orgasm is good enough to sustain a 40-year marriage. In short, you can have a wonderful, satisfying sex life with the person of your dreams, but you cannot measure how much someone will fill your heart by how many orgasms they give you.

How about this definition, Love like life is not a constant variable. It is a shingle of a sliver. Shiny, bright and untarnished.

Love, depending on which professional connoisseur or happily married couple you ask, can be described as a man-made solution for the tumultuous wave of emotions we cannot account for or a force of nature that like the weather we cannot command, demand of or take away. On the other hand, one might describe it as a sudden confluence of emotions in reaction to the sight, sound or smell of a certain individual.

We as humans do have some limited basis to control the weather. We can shelter ourselves from it, embrace it or acclimate ourselves to it. Just as we can seduce, stage a seduction, begin a courtship, the results tend to be dependent on you and the other party.

Love can be a tornado. It invites itself and we cannot dictate how, when or where it tends to touch down. We can choose to surrender to its vestal whims or not. It is hard, like lightening, capricious and incontrovertible. Like finding yourself loving someone, you find detestable.

The more biblical term of love is *"Do unto others as you would have others do unto you"* The democracy founders, the Greeks had the formidable good sense to break love into four levels Kinship, Friendship, Divine, and Sexual. Otherwise known as *"Storge"*, *"Philia"*, *"Agape"* and *"Eros"*.

Storge is reserved for family love, the kind we show for our parents, brother, sister, niece, uncle etc. Sometimes, exceptional friends are included. The movie "Thelma and Louise" is a great example.

Philia is brotherly love or charitable love guided by our preferences.

Agape is love by choice or faith. Normally it is unconditional and related to our love for a deity.

Lastly, but not least is *Eros*. The etymology of erotic. Which is the physical and sexual desire related to intercourse. This also leads to the language of Love.

We all speak the language of love, some more than others and some less enthusiastic than none.

Here are some synopses of the language called love:

- **AFFIRMATION OF CHOICE:** We all are capable of making our assumptions to declare our true intentions to our spouse or partner. If you can't then you should not only check your resentment levels but your relationship status.

- **ENGAGE IN PHYSICAL CONTACT:** Engaging in Physical contact does not necessarily mean sexual intercourse. It could just mean going for a walk as a couple or eating out at his or her favourite restaurant or just hiking.

- **ACTING IN SERVICE TO YOUR SPOUSE:** Doing our best to understand our partner and you will be surprised that he or she is doing their best to understand you. It would definitely give you a kick to a conscious and purposeful relationship. Remember, Loving someone is not a track meet but a cross-country marathon.

- **GIVING PRESENTS:** Doing the laundry, balancing the shared housing incidental account, or cutting the hedges can be more appreciative than the gift of flowers or jewellery. Missing the earlier morning rush to work to see your spouse smile or kissing them out of the blue can be very appreciative.

- **QUALITY TIME TO SHARE:** Making time to spend with that special someone is not a chore.

But hey, why am I defining love?

Is it possible to define LOVE in general?

In my view, LOVE cannot be defined or explained. If it could, it would have a plethora and even a miasma of definitions.

Love is a force of nature, inherently compassionate and emphatic. A dynamic force we cannot command, demand, or exclude, anymore than we can command the moon or the sun to come and go at our whims. Even if we have some constrained proficiency to control the weather, we do so at the chance of disturbing the ecological balance, we also have no control over. In the same manner, we cannot stage a seduction or coordinate a courtship with equitable conclusions, because the resulting outcome might be infatuation or the illusion of love.

Love is a much much larger equation, question, emotion, or chemical confluence than we can contemplate. We can attract love, but we cannot influence how when or where it chooses to express itself. We can choose to surrender to it or not but in the end, like cupids arrow, it strikes capriciously and indubitably, like lightning. Like the sun, Love radiates dispassionately over our uncertainties and aspirations, approaching with conditions, provisos, and appendices. It can make you stupid, brilliant, cowardly, or courageous.

Love is without substance, neither is it a commodity or a merchandisable power resource. Love is intrinsically free of charge. It has no territories, borders, or quantifiable mass. We cannot buy, sell, or trade it. We cannot force or make someone love you, neither can you prevent it, no matter the amount of money. Legislating love or imprisoning it will be at your own peril.

Of course, you can buy sex companions or even marriage spouses. Marriage is the consequence of Love. Orgasms, loyalty, sexual stimulation, and gratification by way of sex toys or just plain fucking can be bought but not love.

Love is a divinity that springs like an arrow from a bow with no doubts, freely from the heart. A willingness of spirit that cannot be turned on or off at the flick of a button. Only something else imitating love can be manipulated as an imitation tactics, be insinuated used as a lure.

Love can be rarely seen these days but it clandestinely speaks out for justice, points out the consequences of hurting oneself and others. It has room for anger, pain and grief and lets them be expressed or released as the owner wishes.

Through love, we are all interconnected. It shows us the sovereignty of our souls. In short, Love is its own commandment.

How did I do? Any closer to knowing what the definition of love is? No, good. Let us put it on the back burner then.

A Love ... sorry, my apologies ... your love, when you succeed in finding it, will be exceptionally different from any others. For you, Love should be the crucial principle that may give way to the beginnings of a marriage or it ought to be.

Maybe we should forget about what love is and ask a better one. What does love mean for you?

However, for a more anal and unambiguous notation here are some suggestions on the explicit definitions of love.

WHAT DOES LOVE MEAN TO YOU?

- Is it a progressive emotion of affection and/or pleasure for a certain individual?
- Could it be an item or entity that provides you with a warm fondness?
- Maybe you don't have it in your heart to love anything. I assure you, that is not the case. No matter the heart, there will be something or someone your heart will beat fast for.
- Could it be a deep sensation for a finite perception other than a person?
- Maybe and it should be a progressive emotion of affection and/or pleasure for a certain individual.

IS LOVE FOREVER?

- The Hollywood drama troupe will have us believe that "Love is forever". They press the fact that no matter what obstacle is present within the machinations of true love, love will certainly and always endure. That is Hollywood. It is a comforting fantasy and one that I somewhat ascribe to. As comforting as this might be, there are situations where love is doomed and more times than not, it does fail.
- That brings us to the *"heart of the matter"*. I tend to believe that we all are asking the wrong question. We shouldn't be questioning "Is Love forever?" rather we should be asking, "How long is forever loving?"
- Philosophically nothing lasts forever and neither does love. This is a conundrum since we pledge ourselves with the words Love for all time. It would make sense though if the human mind were somehow able to last eons, unfortunately the focused human need of greed, power and other endeavours dictates that any relationship will end given enough time.
- In the case of religions and the love of money, love can cause war. For the love of a beautiful face, Troy was destroyed. If Love can make an empire fall on its knees, it can cause men and women to indulge themselves in the seven deadly sins. It can make men steal, murder, commit suicide, shatter marriages, immerse themselves in all sorts of evil.
- Unconditional love is much more better or believable concept than forever love. Unconditional love does not necessarily mean immersing all your hopes, dreams, cares and love into one solitary person. It means harmonising your own well-being and happiness with someone that conversely makes both your lives better.

RECOMMENDATION 10

LET'S TALK ABOUT SEX

> *"Sexiness wears thin after a while, and beauty fades. But to be married to someone who makes you laugh every day, ah, now that's a real treat."*

We all know what sex is but at the same time, we all have different definitions for how we perceive sex. Some regard it as cheap and inflammatory. Some consider it as a pastime, a plaything. Others regard it as sacred. In most opinions, love "should" play a huge distinction when it comes to the act of sex, but regrettably, we have cheapened it with not only our common vices but also our unusual ones. Personally, sex should be a reminder that all things do equal one and that in all our complexities and disappointments, we are unique.

Sex, in my view will and always will be tricky. Sex can be dangerous because it opens the heart to trust, companionship and all the things that make people bond but in some other cases, it can threaten. Besides worrying about pernicious diseases, the fear of pregnancies, couple's desires, wills and don'ts, the shades of other realms, sex is a complicated bastard.

Then again, sex is only an integral part of how we perceive ourselves before marriage. We are all sexual beings, even those relationships that sex does not play a part can be regarded as sexual even if the sexual component is non-existent. As for the act of sex, it should be bone crushingly exquisite and treasured for that brief period of time.

Sex or sexuality is more than the sum of our body parts and the proclivity of sexual intercourse. It includes the intimate touch, affection, empathy, ecstasy, or sorrow we experience and is expressed in our everyday sexual actions. It is our gender identity of the species, our core selves if you will. The sum of how we perceive our image, the shape of our self-esteem and our sexual experiences. A poor body image may have a profound effect on anyone's ability to have a fruitful relationship. For example, a man or woman with a stutter or a personal impediment may think they do not deserve a good sexual partner and might be willing to settle for someone contrary to their true selves.

In short, sex and our sexuality is a fundamental part of who we are, what we are, what we believe, and how we feel in relation to others. For women it is a different matter. Women believe their juices are drying up after the age of forty-five. Some earlier than that. I do not believe that. It is my contention that, women will be women until their early sixties and beautiful women or women who think they are beautiful dry out much faster and earlier than those who are not.

Many people struggle on how to talk honestly about what they need from a partner in and out of bed. Especially women. It is generally understandable that Fathers will not and cannot teach their daughters about sex while mothers are kind of germophobic when it comes to discussing sex with any of their children. Either she fears being seen as promiscuous by her children or the reserved knowledge she knows is not enough. There are specific things many women really want in bed that aren't common knowledge. Most guys do not bother asking what she needs because maybe she's too shy to speak outright about it.

Granted, it's not that easy talking about how or what you really want in bed. For some, the timing is not right or the partner doesn't seem right for that conversation. I know of one female who became so reckless that she blurted what she wanted in the middle of her honeymoon, after vows have been exchanged. Risking everything and possibly putting off the show.

Talking openly about sex and the wide range of hypothetical scenarios between couples before walking down the aisle is a most worthwhile thing to do. Marriage changes a sex life and its habits in ways that cannot be anticipated.

We are never taught the intricacies of having a constructive conversation about sex and considering your age, circumstance and your inclination, the sex conversation before marriage is uncomfortable to you. It brings to mind the time you learnt about "the birds and the bees" from the girl's bathroom door or the time you learnt about where the zucchini goes from the locker room walls or when your best friend explained how babies were made. All that being true, nevertheless, the sex talk with your partner has to be had, because a spouse's inherent requirements are not obvious at the start of a relationship especially when love factors affect the novelty and thrill of sex. Not talking about sex and your preferences with your spouse before the big day may lead to sexual frustration in the long run.

As a special sub-classification of sex, your partner should be up for everything and anything, as many times as possible in one sitting. He or she has to be between fair and impressive and be able or willing to try new things. Without making the effort to try new things, sex can get routinely boring rather quickly. Trying new things isn't about the trying, it is about the sense of adventure they both explore. Don't be prudish, take lessons, and learn. I'm sure you can work that out. Remember age, size or shape doesn't necessarily have a limit.

With the options provided by social media, sexual gratification and stimulation whether by way of fingers, toys, orally, chains and whips or plain intercourse can now be bought, sold or given.

I don't believe in virginity or the notion of a "Purity Pledge" or any of that nonsense. These days, sex is more like filling the empty spaces in our hearts. The idea where youths take out a pledge to abstain from sex until they are married or till their adults, when they are best able to handle the ramifications of sex is admirable and yet unfulfilling. Safe sex, even oral sex has its consequences and tends to result in the wrong answers. My suggestion to them is best you do the deed before you say, "I do".

There is a scenario where neither companion or perhaps one-half of a couple does not have the capacity or know the extent of their own sexual drive. In either case, it is best they explore it and find out for themselves their innate desires.

When it comes to sex before marriage, most couples do not want to wait until the honeymoon. How would they feel if the sex wasn't up to par that first night in the bedroom after the vows? Having sex before marriage is the more established way to gauge the sexual compatibility between couples. Beware of the fact that because you have mind-blowing sex before marriage does not necessarily mean it will continue. Imagine one partner charged with a crime or having cancer or has an accident and goes blind. The scenarios are endless, hence the conversation before marriage. Once the silence around a sexual issue has been broken there is an intense relief, a more secure and optimistic sexual future to look forward to. Taking vows could dampen the sexual compatibility between couples because our bodies naturally age or change with time and life events.

WHY PREMARITAL SEX IS ADVISED:

YOUR INDIVIDUALITY: Knowing your true sexual predilections has to be acknowledged, first by yourself then your partner. You do not want to wake up ten years into the marriage and find out you have yearnings for someone with the same sex as you. Unfortunately, this advice is somewhat redundant because even now people who have been married 30 years still find it hard to acknowledge that they are gay or straight. To you and them ... I say *"Know Thyself"* before a great undertaking like marriage is done.

SENSUAL INTERACTION: Otherwise known as sexual chemistry is something that can only be determined by, well ... having sex. Our minds and bodies want different things when it comes to sex. It's best you find out how compatible you both are before the wedding than after. No one wants to find out that they only have great sex after they've had a few drinks or after he or she knocks them about a bit or after an argument.

SEX, THE EVENT: Are you a good listener or responder to the reactions of your partners responses. A spouse could be lousy in bed with the wrong partner and just simply magnificent with the right one. Not all of us are great in bed, we don't start great at all. That comes with heeding to the responses of your spouse. The objective of sex before marriage is to become sexually empowered, expressive, unperturbed and confident. Knowing what makes you feel good in your skin, knowing the wants, the needs and desires that both turn you on and off.

ISSUES: Sexual Issues before marriage cannot be left to fate. It is one of the conditions of marriage. A marriage is not a marriage until it is consummated. Just as partners discuss children, politics, religion, and family before marriage they have to discuss their sexual issues. There is a certain curiosity about whether or not you and your partner are on the same page, sexually. There might be several sexual problems you both have not considered. Impossible as it may sound, you might have an allergic reaction to your partner's semen. He might have a premature ejaculation problem. She maybe infertile. He has an impotency issue or perhaps she has a non-squirting problem. These might be some of the sexual concerns both spouses have to address before marriage.

THE SIZE: Most women are curious about the size of their partner's package the instant they start dating. That's why they have a right to know what's down there. It is a healthy curiosity, because nobody likes unusual surprises. Would you want to know your fiancé is packing a bent freckled howitzer or a straight automatic? Men on the other hand are concerned with the boobs of women. Fortunately, they have front row seats to the love bags.

WHY PREMARITAL SEX IS NOT ADVISABLE:

LOSS OF INTEREST: Sometimes both men and women lose sexual interest with wives or husbands after tying the knot. Maybe because of the stable sex diet they receive before and after the vows are said.

HEALTH: Health related issues might occur prior to the marriage. Problems that may relate to intercourse or the everyday life of one partner may affect the future of the marriage.

FULFILMENT: The attraction and physical fulfilment sometimes do not last long after marriage. Both husband and wife, after their vows may feel that giving their entire being to one individual is unfulfilling, that there may be nothing left to look forward to in regards to their lives.

THE MYTH: The myth of having a partner soon wears off after marriage mainly because of their previous experiences before the vows. The reason being the libido or the intimacy shown during the initial phases of the relationship.

RECOMMENDATION 11

FEEDING THE WRONG WOLF

"Life isn't perfect but love doesn't care"

Your happiness will be like feeding one of the two wolfs that lie within. You have to figure which of the two wolves you will be feeding. Two similar wolves that look alike but within one is white and exceptional, promoting goodwill and good tidings while the other is grey and mangy inside, long-winded and starved. Which of the two you feed most would be the cradle of your relationship. Unfortunately, with both wolves appearing very much alike despite their appearance, you never know which one to feed.

Someone once asked me 'When do you know marriage is the next step?'

I answered rather acerbically, 'When you cannot afford not to go through it'

Your happiness is relative and if you find you are happy with your partner and your present circumstances without being married, I suggest you don't rock the boat. Rock the boat only when you feel like it would not only improve your happiness but it would make you a better person because of it.

Please Note:

- What generally should make partners happy is engaging with each other in a very positive social interaction with others and having sex.
- "Happily ever after" is a reality, though a rarely distinct phenomenon. If or when you arrive at this spot, if you're happy with your marriage do not question the means by which you arrived at that spot. You are happy and that should be the end of it.
- We all dream of having that 5-carat bling slipped on our left ring fingers because others send us reeling into that feeling of marriage bliss of asking ourselves "When will it be my turn?". However, despite our relationships and our desires we should understand that getting married isn't in itself the all and end of having what we truly desire or being happy.

When traditions, the populace and instincts combine to advocate that not getting married means something is seriously defective with us, it can be a difficult concept to process, especially I think with women.

Granted research does suggest that married couples are much happier than those who aren't, it only suggests that they are happier because of the good relationships they have we those around them. Much like when sparks fly between divorced couples after a failed marriage.

FINDING THAT PERFECT PARTNER

Finding that perfect someone is sometimes based on luck. All the same, you are more likely to find your partner in either your everyday activity, clubbing or vacationing. Depending on your interests, your attitudes towards yourself and others. Do try to resist, the temptation to leave finding your soulmate to faith.

Here are some tips on how to attract that special soulmate of yours.

1) **NURTURE YOUR DESIRABLE CHARACTERISTICS**:

   Within yourself, you can find a list of traits in you that would be appealing to a partner. Maybe you have a nice smile and a pleasant sense of humour. Work on yourself and you might end up meeting that somebody who shares your interest and desires. No matter what your list of positive traits, consider how a potential partner might be able to personify those traits and utilise them to your own benefit. Of course, you might not end up meeting that special someone but you have definitely improved yourself and enhanced your traits for that casual meeting you might have someday. It is also possible that you will be attracted to someone who exhibits a different sort of attributes and vice versa. This is fine, not everyone is alike.

2) **KEEP AN OPEN MIND**:

   There are few personality quirks that are objectionable in your search for that soulmate. That is normal, let your instincts guide you more that your own list of ideal peculiarities you hope to find in your soulmate. Avoid passing judgement and certain biases or prejudices like skin colour, religion, age. Take your time to know the idiosyncrasies of that person with an open mind. You just might find yourself being surprised by those quirks.

3) **GIVE INVOLVED INDIVIDUALS A WIDE BERTH**:

   There is a covenant relationship with married couples. The allure of meeting someone already in a relationship is enticing to some of us. There is no doubt the sex is great and the inconsistent state of sneaking off to that clandestine rendezvous is enthralling. The whiff of vulnerability carries an

Before the "I Dos" & Other Compendiums

irresistible urge for us to be ferocious, either in the bedroom or with the act of sleuthing. Rooted in the scarcity of wanting what we can't have is primal. It is best you wait until your ideal partner is single, providing you with a fighting chance of a positive relationship or better still, try and put him or her out of your mind and focus on someone else. Would you want your spouse sneaking off behind your back to meet a lover, huh!? Your choice.

4) **BE PATIENT**:

Patience is a virtue. Wooing a partner takes time. When courting someone you need to be patient. There is a duality of neediness in an intimate relationship with yourself and your hypothetical mate. Applying patience as a tool will be the test to deepen your relationship.

5) **DEVELOP YOUR SOCIAL INTERACTIONS**:

Facebook, Twitter, Instagram, and all other social media apps are now the modern day equivalent of arrange marriages and the village matchmaker. The more you expand your social network, the more your dating pool swells. The online dating world is a rough world to navigate but when creating your dating profile you have to be honest but leave enough room in it to be enigmatic and brief. Your profile should be as vague as is necessary, it's not wise to show all your cards right away. Having that coffee or drink on your get-togethers face-to-face is when the chips have to fall and you both get to know each other.

On the other hand, that is not the only way to meet likeminded people. If you want to meet new exciting, likeminded and auspicious people, pursue friendships and acquaintances, join a convenient social group, volunteer for causes you believe in. If you can, host dinner parties or schedule an informal happy hour.

6) **GO ON BLIND DATES**:

Most of us dread blind dates. Unfortunately, if you are on the prowl for that soul mate of yours, going on blind dates is part of increasing your dating pool. It's a necessary step to open yourself to opportunities that get you to meet interesting people. Your mother, your friends know you and some of your preferences. Let their instincts guide you towards a good match. Probably won't, but hey ... you never know.

7) **GET OUT OF YOUR COMFORT ZONE**:

On occasion, the intermittent flow of adrenaline stimulates arousal in someone you are not likely to be attracted to. Visiting a place where you are not likely to visit could stimulate your senses into an advantageous position. Sweating, having a fast heartbeat might make you experience extreme emotions. Could make you more susceptible to sexual attraction. Gyms, a cinema playing a horror film or high towers are likely places to experience such a feeling.

8) **BE FRIENDLY**:

It goes without saying "You attract more bees with honey than vinegar". A smile and laugh will make new acquaintances feel comfortable around you. Your come-hither body language, coupled with your openness, will encourage some light flirtation and in turn, will provide a great way to determine your response. Is he or she attracted to you? Can you be attracted to him or her as well?

9) **IMPROVE YOUR FLIRTING LINGO**:

Flirting is the most audacious sport in the world. If it were an Olympic game, there would not be a referee capable of umpiring it. That is because flirting is a combination of several emotionalist functions. First though, you need to be knowledgeable about topics you might not want to be conversant about. You have to be courteous, communicative, complimentary and be capable of use a friendly open body language. Try not to be closed off, try not to show off, and try not to be a self-depreciative egomaniac or a teaser. Those are no no's when it comes to flirting. To flirt successfully you must be able to listen and affirm conversations with nods or verbal agreements, continue the conversations, make eye contact, ask and pose questions. And at all times express yourself through your open palms, arms, and legs. Not that it works all the time but it does open other doors.

10) **ENJOY YOUR ELIGIBILITY:**

You are single and have a great life. Good for you. You probably have interesting hobbies, know the value of friendship and family, have a stable and promising career, what else do you need? You need someone to share your life, your goals, and beliefs. It is counterintuitive, but it is important to be content and confident as you are before you go running off to find that soulmate of yours. Relationships are successful if both partners are healthy, stable, and confident in themselves. Knowing who you are and what you are is the first step in launching yourself into the world of dating.

Post Script:

It is advisable that you always keep a journal. A chronicle of your activities will help keep you focused and remind you of your goals and how far you have come.

RECOMMENDATION 12

AND FINALLY ... YOUR LOVE

"Love is not a noun; it's a verb. It isn't something you buy. It's something you give and receive everyday"

"Money is what makes the world go round" sayeth that popular philosopher. I beg to differ. *"Love is what should make the world go round"*. At least it should be. If we truly have love in our hearts then the world should be a loving place.

We all think of love as the "be it! and all end of happiness". That may be true, but it is also different to each of us and has a convergence of wonderful tickly emotions. Some see it as a quandary, an impractical reaction, with irrational actualities and an inexplicable desire that is illogical in all its complexities.

Scientists consider love as a biochemical collision of molecules that occurs due to emotional changes in the body. A short term, continually emotion that can at times sustain a marriage. A somewhat yearning of an idealised passion that could be characterised as love or a blood-tie of affinity. Alternatively, as one scientist put it *"a micro-moment of positive resonance"*.

Obviously, these scientists have not been in love before.

In Cain and Abel's time, love or the idea of love was not considered a factor. 500 years ago, it was considered a taboo or insanity. Today love can be seen on almost every street corner and home. Or so we think.

A friend once defined his love as "Loving, being loved and being in love, regardless". Nice huh? Here can be another description of your love. "Love is putting someone else's feeling and needs before your own". A specific attraction to the virtuous, feelings, flaws and imperfections of a precise individual.

Both are very good definitions.

Here is what in my view, society today has made with the definition of all of our love; "Love is Pain". Loving anyone or anything is hard. It isn't as clean as hate. The act of Loving, like anything in life is a difficult road to trudge.

Your love should be knowing that the person across from you will be there even in the roughest of times and you for them. Someone who could look you in the eye for twenty minutes and not shy away or blink without the weight of a heavy conscience. Having said that, there are only two true delineations of love most scholars adhere to. Love is honesty between partners and hard work. Bear in mind, that literal truth is colossally different from honesty of the heart. The other most common of circumstances regarding "True Love" is that it is unrequited. Love is sometimes complicated. At other times, it's not. True love notwithstanding.

Yes, I'm a cynic when it comes to true love. It's just a belief I have. We all have our own definition of love. Yours is the best one to follow. It is a basic rule that all human's, always lie about the basic emotions or feelings we have. Love notwithstanding.

Naturally, I know that some couples believe they are truly in love, well good for them. That said, if you are hesitant, there are simple ways to find out. (See Below)

LOVE FOR WOMEN

Chemistry, red-hot sex, and partnership are respectable basis for any good marriage and I'll encourage you to seek these in your future life partner. You need to know what kind of partner, be it man or woman, you are promising yourself to. Here are some guidelines.

Appraise him with your head, not just your heart:

In the course of the Velcro stage of relationships, you may habitually converge on the assured and neglect or make apologies for the deleterious. Be as distinct and unbiased when evaluating a potential partner as you would if you were contracting a nanny for your child.

Shoulder to Cry On:

Love is always being affectionate, sympathetic, accepting and inspirational. These should be all the positive check marks on any list.

Anyone's love Life will be beset with deviations enough to make anyone heads spin.

Men especially have a hard time of it and will need all the fondness and physical bond from someone to hold onto. Yes, sometimes they have the need to be grouchy, they are allowed. As long as it is not a permanent mood of theirs.

Men's Concerns:

For men, marriage is not his foremost concern. Their concern is how many women they can score with before they need to go shopping for a wedding ring. They always wonder within themselves on how long they can evade that big noose around the neck, called a marriage. Men do not fear commitment, they dread it.

Before the "I Dos" & Other Compendiums

When men hear those five little words, "Why don't we get married", their chest tightens and they get all dizzy. Especially, if they are in a long-term relationship.

When a man feels comfortable with the notion of marriage, only then will his reasons for marriage be yours. He will succumb to the trappings and go for it wholeheartedly.

Is He the Considerate Sort?:

Tender-hearted is he, Huh? Men do not like to be considered cissies. Men, like to be refered to as gritty and manly. Any man who doesn't like that has something else in his bag of tricks.

No woman can truly answer what kind of man she is pursuing? Is he a tough lover, a puzzler, a compassionate one or is he one with serial killer instincts, a Machiavellian person, or a Johnny be Goode farmer? You just hope they know.

Here is a way that might illuminate the puzzle. Does he make time for you? Does he do small needless things for you?

A man's tongue is the most infectious disease there is for a woman. You cannot help believe his truths and lies, If he whispers in the right way or curve his lips in just the way you like, your heart skips a beat, you would be a fool not to kiss him to death. As his smile emanates from his heart so does yours. It could turn cold or hot at a moment's notice.

Are Your Ideals Comparable?:

We all have a symbiotic relationship with the world and how we treat is says much about who we are than who we are not. Does he share your need of volunteering for the helpless, your vacationing in inhospitable places, camping, your job or your Musical collection or whatever you are into? Your values do not have to align with each other but they do to be appreciated.

Are Your Ambitions Similar?:

Go-getting men are a godsend, they also, unfortunately, have a Self-absorbed ideals. Their focus does not easily alter and may fall foul of your future.

His vision will take president over all priorities. If you concur with his vision, oh what a twosome you will be.

Do you think he's Empathetic?

Co-operation is a good way to set in motion your partnership. His effort in pleasing your interests means he treasures you. It may be in small ways but at least he appreciates you. Be sure to respond to his efforts and show your gratitude since feelings taken for granted can easily lead to bitterness or other undesirable reactions. His endeavours do diminish after some time but that doesn't mean he doesn't care. His efforts to support you should not have to diminish. So do not let it.

Pay attention to how you feel when you are with him:

Does your time with him leave you with greater self-esteem and more zest to connect with people and projects outside the relationship? If the opposite is true, consider whether the relationship is good for you. If phone calls or time together leaves you feeling diminished or down, move on.

LOVE FOR MEN

You need to know what kind of partner, be it woman or man, you are pledging yourself to. Here are some guidelines.

Her appearance:

Society defines beauty for us, especially to the males of our generation. Each man is attracted to a certain type of woman that possesses his own personal eccentricities. Strangely, a woman fits a certain image of beauty for a particular sort of man to be interested in her for matrimony, but take away the clothes, wipe off the make-up and cut off the hair and you'll see a different image of that beauty.

"Beauty" among women is high priority, that is why one in six women would rather have a nest of vipers camped out in their handbag than suffer a breakout of spots. Some will refuse to be photographed if they have not put on any make-up or have bad skin, because they know a pretty face will get the best of men anytime. So be careful of the comments you make to your partner. Make sure that your definition of beauty fits what you see as beautiful.

Is She Kindhearted?

Kindhearted? Huh. Is she Kindhearted? Not all women are filled with sugar and spice. A woman who comes across as kindhearted may have salt in her pocket and vinegar smeared on her lips. You will never know. No man can truly answer this. They just hope they know. Here is a way that might illuminate the puzzle. Does she do small unnecessary things for you or for some other reason? Maybe for her? A woman's smile is the most infectious disease there is. You cannot help smiling back at her smile. Her smile can clean up your savings, make your soul turn in on itself or please you in ways you never thought possible. If her smile emanates from her heart then you would be a fool to give her a pass. That is what I know about this subject. Thankfully, this is a parameter you could probably give up.

Are Your Values Similar?

The way we treat the world around us is important. They stem from our upbringings and what we learn along the way. Does she share your camping holidays or your DVD collection or your Marathon drive or whatever floats your boat? Because it does not matter how attractive to one another or even how extraordinary well you get along if your values do not align the future will not be bright at all.

Are Your Ambitions Similar?

Ambitious women are a godsend they also, unfortunately have a tigers tail. Her vision of the future will not alter because of your goals and dreams. She has her vision and she will chase it with an insatiability like the one you have never seen. She can take on the world and you, if you get in her way. Good for you. She will be partner in love and life if you do not stand in her way.

Is She Supportive?

Give and take is a good way to start-off with, provided it goes both ways. Her putting effort in your interests or something else means she values you. It may be in a small way but at least she appreciates you. Be sure to reciprocate her efforts and show your appreciation because feelings taken for granted can easily lead to resentments or other negative reactions. At any rate, in longer relationships the effort does somewhat diminish. It should not have to. So do not let it.

Intelligently Challenging:

Her appearance is what men go for initially. However, beauty is only skin-deep. It is difficult to spot a woman with a brain from across a crowded room. In contrast, a warm and sincere voice is worth a face with a broken shield. Will her conversations and attitude be intellectually challenging as her appearance? If it is, then her mind will triumph her appearance now and in the future.

Good sense of Humor:

Having a relatively good sense of humor is always an asset. For a man or a woman. If you have a sense of humor, let us hope your partner appreciates it. If it is lost on her, it will cause tension. She will be serious, perhaps become annoyed at the slightest use of your humor and even become resentful. It is necessary for a couple to be playful with each other, it lightens the mood and periodically extends having fun together. Laughter never gets old, does it?

Sociable and friendly:

Having someone by your side for events is always a good thing. No man or woman wants to be apprehensive about the person they love by his or her side embarrassing them. He or she does not need to be angry with them or turns their nose at them. They would rather have a colleague in all parts of his or her life. Needless to say, she would possess all the qualities that make her a passable hostess and extend the same courtesy that is passed on to her.

Understanding and affectionate:

Love is having to be affectionate, considerate, accepting and inspiring. If you are making a checklist, this should be among your top ranked yeses on your worksheet. Life is full of vicissitudes enough to make heads spin. Couples especially have a hard time and will need all the fondness and physical bond offered, like a shoulder to cry on, hand holding, hugs, sex and love they have and more. Yes, sometimes you have the need to be grouchy, you are allowed. As long as it is not a permanent mood of yours.

SUGGESTIONS FOR WOMEN .... On what they should never say, do or let their significant other know.

"You're the smallest guy I've ever been with…, but it's okay!":

Imagine comparing him to your ex. No insult like, "Your dick is small but I'm really into you" is so damaging to a man than any other. It is a major slap in the face and a complete mood demolisher. No amount of seductive prodding would ever get that constant ringing denigration out of his head. Unless you intentionally want to be responsible for making your spouse/fiancée completely self-conscious, do not say or even imply this. It would be better if you castrated him instead.

"Oh it's only a water bra":

You've padded your bra. Well, good for you. Let him believe they are real. Men are simple-minded. A little white lie won't hurt him and a hint of ambiguity in your sex lives would not hurt either one of you. But hey, when he learns the truth, please soft pedal it.

You tell him you are having your period:

The literate male has a basic understanding of how the female reproductive cycle operates. Probably aced sex-education in high school. So he understands the principle of you getting your period. Yes, he gets it, he just doesn't need to hear or know about it. Even if there's an ugly scene happening in your panties, please for heaven sakes, keep it to yourself. The only information he needs to know is that "It's that time of the month". That is enough of a detail he is willing to bear.

"Damn it, I'm feeling so bloated today":

Most men miss the day in sex education of one colossal foremost factor. Cotton candy does not come out of girls. Girls, do shit too. They too, have upset stomachs, have to relieve themselves and go to the toilet. I know, it's shocking. What –? Brook Shields, Britney, Madonna? They get shit-faced and plug up toilets too? Ok, so you are feeling a little flush in the downstairs department. It doesn't mean you should go off flaunting your flatulence to your man. He knows you go, but at the same time, he doesn't need to know you go. Catch my drift?

"What do you think scented or unscented tampons?":

Whether your tampons smell like sweet fresh bread, heaven, freshly baked pie or otherwise, no man wants to hear about it. It simply grosses them out. They are likely to squirm at the thought of the subject.

"You're not usually my type":

All girls have fallen for that guy outside of their comfort zone. He may be duller, thinner, less adventurous, less handsome, too much of a coward or less burlier than your normal guy may. Someone that you would never look twice at. Under normal circumstances, we can't help whom we fall for. It's unlikely you would understand if your spouse informed you that he normally goes for blonde-haired women or dimpled brunettes. Yeah, I didn't think so ...

"If you loved me, you would know":

Such a statement is as ambiguous as it is misleading. It forces him to prove his love to you by testing him. How would you feel if he said the same thing to you? Most men have learnt that this is a female mind game of some sort and it disgusts them to think otherwise. It is a bad idea to play games with someone you are about to marry.

You tell him "I'm fine":

Oh yeah you are, but you are not. Most men do not have the sensitivity to know whether their spouses are fine or not. If you are as intimate as you think you are, he can probably see the emotional turmoil underneath and he might know you are not your usual self. In any case, he will or will not enquire fully, until you verbalised the crisis. Men have a fastidious nature when it comes to a woman's pain. As it is, everyone else knows you are not fine, even your friends know you are not fine. There is no need to play games. Something is bothering you, do not wait for him to figure out because, hey breaking news, he already knows.

Do not ask if he thinks that girl is pretty:

Admit it. You don't really want to know the truth. If you do, then it's just possible you are setting him up for failure. That is just cruel and unusual punishment and very irresponsible of you. In addition, it is just a little patronising. It will as hell baffle the heck out of your spouse.

Do not press the question, "What's wrong? Are you sure? Tell me what's wrong":

Some men at heart are bachelors and tend to protect and enjoy their space religiously. Out of concern, you can inquire of him what is wrong but do not bug him, hoping he will cave. He might or he might not. It is most likely that he will get angry or go into a field of desperation or depression. Never mind, when he wants to share he will. But he won't if you nag him constantly.

"I do not like your friends":

There is being honest and then there is just being mean. And insensitive. Do not rip on his boys unless you have a legit reason, 'kay ladies?

"When we're married…"

Never start a statement like that. If you guys have been dating for, like, four months and begin to talk about the future that has not really happened, just... don't. Men fear the "M" word like Americans fear the mad-cows disease. Above all, he fears commitment. He'll most likely avoid you or run away scared, no matter how much he digs you if you presume so much. Best you ease him into a state of contentment before your breach the subject of togetherness.

"Do not ask him if you look fat in this?"

In the history of questions, this might be a guy's least favourite question. Men never know the right answer, but in some stage of your relation, they expect and fear their answer, because they know it is a trick question and no matter what answer they give, it will never be the one you expect. Girl, you do not look fat. Cut it out.

Stop asking, "Who was that on the phone?":

He is not a baby and you are not his mother. Social messaging is the new age conversational appliance. Yeah, girl you can text all day and night but for some reason he is not allowed to answer the phone or receive text messages. Of course, he's allowed to get text messages and speak to a female over the phone without you looking over his shoulder to know whom they're from. Please lady, do not be so insecure. Grow up.

SUGGESTIONS FOR MEN .... On what they should never say, do or let your significant other know.

"Are you having your PMS?"

Never ask. Women get a little crazy when Mother Nature's curse comes a-knocking. That does not mean they're going to fess up to it when you ask. Simply don't ask or question them when the impending doom of "Eve's Curse" comes about.

Do not tease her unnecessarily:

Women are sensitive and usual playful banter must cease in due course. A watered-down version of this banter may take its place sure, but learn when to put the brakes on because you never know when she might take something you say jokingly to heart. Inadvertent transgressions are at a high risk during a playful time and can bring cause for World War in your home.

Do not let her get full control the remote:

The television in the home is like Switzerland. It is the holy grail of the living room. You guys watch the sports and/or the movies with your mates. It's also, where you sit to watch the documentaries or movies you both agree or disagree on. You do not want to sit through a box set of "Sex in the City", "Bridget Jones Diary" or the next episode of "Grey's Anatomy" if you do not want to. All the same, there are times when she will want to watch "This is Us" and bawl her eyes out. You should probably not fight her on it. Hell, you just might enjoy that.

Pass judgment:

Intervening and passing judgement on her when she is being uncooperative, especially if she is pregnant or during that time of the month is not advisable. The best offense sometimes is to do nothing. A friend's girlfriend prepared a meal for herself that consisted of a peanut butter and meaty crisp sandwich with eggnog. Because she was pregnant at the time, my friend averted his eyes and continued doing the accounts. It was worth it.

Do not let her know the number of times you have gotten laid:

Hell yeah, all men love bragging about their conquests, real or make-believe. Then again, giving your current lover or spouse a tally of that number is very boorish. Yes, we all know you're no virgin, that does

Before the "I Dos" & Other Compendiums

not mean your betrothed wants to know details of your triumphs. If you are the kind of guy who cannot help bragging, then you had better reconsider your life choices.

It is not advisable to let her know your annual salary:

Yes, your annual salary can be described as enviable. Hurrah for you, there is no need to scream it from the rooftops. At the other end of the spectrum, if your income is not that privileged, still shield her from the details. Men are very conscious and could be envious of the differences between their partner's remunerations and theirs, especially if they are not exactly the breadwinner. In any case, if your other half is awfully or unusually paying too much attention to your monetary details, then beware you might be dealing with what Kanye West calls a "Gold-digger".

Your Porn Stash:

Most men, not all, have a porn stashes in various denominations. They love porn. Girls do too, but are very discreet about it. Do not be ashamed of it but be subtle about it. Your partner has no need to view your hoard and would not appreciate your showing it to her, especially if your sphinx-like proclivities deviate sharply from hers. If you do not want her to bicker you endlessly about never hoping to compete with a Jessica Darlin whenever you want to have sex, then my friend never show her your stash. Some women are so axiomatic that they will be so disgusted they will either dump your arse or get rid of your prized collected works when you're not looking.

Your Vulnerabilities:

Maybe you are a sensitive person who volunteers for charity and all those niceness we hope would impress not only ourselves but also those beside us. You cry when DiCaprio finally freezes to death and sinks down into the ocean or with Aniston when she finally gets her man. These are all good characters in a man just as long he is not overly candid about his sensitivities, especially in public. Your partner might find it cute for a while but if she were to make a choice between a brigand and you, she will choose the bandit. Who could blame her? No one wants a weakling or a cry-baby as a spouse.

Your Castles in the air:

Exchanging sexual fantasies could most definitely result in some really heart thumping, hot sweating, mind-blowing sex. Mind, you do not reach for the Castle too often. If you prefer the thought of your babe dressing up as a nurse, a mechanic or an Indian princess before going down on you, then express the idea to her gently. Having said that, if your Castle contains the vision of your woman performing kinkier acts involving sex toys, power tools or whatever, then you might need to solicit your pleasure from other source. Maybe a therapist or some other kind of help. A stripper and/or hooker, for example. Best you keep them to yourself or blow off steam alone in the bathroom with a cold shower.

Masturbation Frequency:

Yes, women know men masturbate, that does not mean they want to know about it or understand why men do it, especially when she is doing her best to pleasure him. You have a partner now. There is no need to *"flog the bishop"* any longer.

The Ex:

Our hearts contain numerous vaults and in one of them are the memories of your torrential or sprightly affairs with previous girlfriends. Lock them up tight and hide the key. Your spouse does not need to dig up old love letters or photos of your ex. No doubt if she finds even one unfamiliar picture or letter of your ex, she will forever use it as ammo and balk at you in future arguments.

What do Women like in Men?

- Women love to hold hands. Even if she says she doesn't, some part of her loves it and especially in public. Besides a guy wants her to be the only hand he wants to hold and she knows it. It is a universal and sadly a primeval indicator that he is hers and she is his. A signal that he is her protector and that he is proud to be hers. She'll never want to let it go.
- When a woman compliments an item of clothing that their partner wears, it is best to take the verbal cue and wear it more.
- Women like it when their partner asks advice from them. It shows that there is trust in the relationship and that she is someone you can count on.
- Women don't like flirty partners. It means he or she isn't a one-woman man.
- Some women like partners they feel can protect them. Preferably, someone with an alpha personality or close. Someone who makes her feel secure and comfortable. However, not to the point of smothering out her ideals, either or both of her opinions.
- Women adore partners who do not only think about sex. And why the hell not. Well because after a while, sex might become a redundant chore of the relationship.
- Women love romantic partners. A partner who wouldn't find it such a chore to kiss her in the rain or on the bus.
- If a woman really wants to be with a specific partner, she'll move mountains, even heaven and earth to make sure that it happens.
- A woman will enjoy a partner if he or she knows her likes and her dislikes. It's a signal that he or she is interested in her and looking forward to a healthy relationship.

What Women Are Not Fond of:

- **The Ex:** Women are not too thrilled with partners who aren't over the Ex.
- **The Other Woman:** Women abhor being compared in any way or fashion to other women.
- **Inattentiveness:** Women have an aversion to phrases like "Can't it wait hon?" They find being ignored insufferable and rude. Do not be rude, they just hate that.
- **Being Bothered:** When a woman doesn't feel good, she does not say much. Leave her be, pushing her buttons into conversation will only result in a mutilated confrontation, you won't be keen on.
- **Her Compassionate Heart:** Never take advantage of a woman's forgiving nature. There is a reason why *"Hell hath no fury like a woman scorned"*. Her heart can take much, but when it reaches breaking point and cracks to smithereens, God help him who reviled her.
- **Men who lie:** We all lie. Small little white lies are harmless. Try not to lie to her. She will always instinctively know it if you are.
- **Reiterations:** Women hate repeating themselves. If you make her repeat something, say an appointment for a fourth, or fifth time, it displays your lack of interest to her.
- **Distrustfulness:** Trust, sometimes can be a woman's chastity belt for her heart. Making her infuriated by not trusting her when she is being honest is a good way for her to distance herself. Once her trust is gone, it's almost impossible to retrieve it again. That is not to say honesty and trust are always ideal in a relationship. Sometimes secrets are what bind a couple or guard them against cynicism. Some secrets need to be kept, whilst some are harmful to others. Secrets sometimes are need to keep a relationship secure. Yes, no matter what they say, women despise being suspicious. But there may come a time of your choosing when all is revealed,

and that time may never come. Trust her if you must, but Samson did trust Delilah, and we know what happened to him.

- **Being Belittled:** Whether they be good or not, women never underestimate their feelings for their spouse and are greatly annoyed when it is denigrated.
- **Egotism:** If a woman dislikes someone, her partner should by default not converse with that person. It may be selfish and disagreeable but it presents a bond between the couple.
- **Dishonesty:** Yes, men by nature get restless and are sometimes eager to explore the forbidden fruits available. Why? Well, it just might provide wonderful distractions to the conflicts in and around the home. Women are repulsed by cheaters and can get very incensed when they find out. So, whatever you do *"Never cheat on her"* no matter how inviting an offer is presented to you. Remember, the *"Hell hath no fury …"* quote, keep that to heart. If you do have to cheat, then do not get caught, which is a very high probability. Remember, cheating is like dining with the devil. Hope he has a long spoon! So *"do not cheat"* on your lover. It's the first matriculated rule when you enter their life.
- **Tawdriness:** Some women are very ostentatious with their looks, while others are the opposite. They sometimes act like drama queens, divas or are very reticence. Take care to appreciate the look but do not address them in the manner they parade in. Just go with the flow and be the partner she needs you to be.
- **Mammoth Clad Vanity:** Most men have an in-built Narcissism complex within their system. It just cannot be helped. This is definitely a turn-off for most women.
- **Pallid Suitors:** Women are innately cautious of men who have any kind of physical or mental detriment. Not only health but emotional instability and personality. Which is silly really, because no man, whoever they are is without

a black mark of sorts on their person, be it in the flesh or emotionally.
- **Disinterest:** Most women cannot stand men who are indifferent when it comes to showing empathy. They can instinctively feel the presence of a cold heart but will ignore it if the fellow they are interested in has a nice arse.

What Do Her Actions or Thoughts Mean?

- The moment a woman starts to shy away from their partners, there is something definitely wrong. Women are very observant of their partner's actions and tend to be furtive in their activities, so they do not get noticed. It's a statistical fact that from losing their make-up kit to the fear of an assault, women suffer the stress of anxiety much more than their male spouses. They are also much more better at concealing their concerns.
- It's a veritable fact that all women always think too much.
- When a woman admits she misses a guy or chick, she really does. Never take that lightly.
- All Chicks flirt. Some more than others. Some don't mean it, while some are definitely trying to provoke a reaction. Nevertheless, at the end of the day she'll be watching the sun go down with the one she truly loves.
- Much like men, women never know what they need, but they do, at times, know what they want.
- Most times women already know the truth of things before they ask their man. So, guys be careful.
- If a woman is still in love with someone else, she'll never say a bad thing against him or her.
- When a woman lays her head on her man's chest, listening to his heartbeat, she is also waiting to see if he will mention what he's thinking.
- When a woman tells her man or woman nothing is wrong, she is lying. Everything is wrong. That is the irony of women.

Before the "I Dos" & Other Compendiums

- Women remember the littlest things the most.
- Women will always give the person they truly love a second, a third … chance.
- When women write love notes to their loved one, that person should keep them.
- If a woman laughs at a person's every joke, even the bad ones, she likes him or her.
- Women sometimes test their partners to see how they'll react.
- When women cuddle or hug their partner tight, they never want to let that moment go.
- When a woman says NO, it either means NO or give me space but keep trying. Women are mercurial when it comes to deciding for a person's interests.
- It's true when a woman says her partner is an important part of her life.
- It's almost true that women never touch potential suitors by accident.
- All women know instinctively when someone is interested in them.
- When a woman wants a mate, she'll get a mate.
- If a woman really cares about someone, you will see it in their eyes.
- When a woman whispers things about what she loves to a suitor, she is falling in love.

What Men Like In the Bedroom:

Modesty is becoming a lost sentiment in today's climate, despite our early memories that teach us to be modest wherever we are. Strip away that humility and you will find that despite protestations, most men want and desire the same things in the bedroom as women. Granted, not many men are interested in bulls, whips, chains, or wax on the nipples kind of sex, but there are many varieties within the "Shades of Grey" community that some men will find a fancy for. What they need from the numerous choices of satisfying their urges can be far docile than any work of fiction. They tend to want the same things most women want but are too shy or afraid to admit. For a relationship to work best, both partners need to break the social niceties between them and explore what they both want in the bed. Trust, Understanding and Gratification. Here are some thoughts about what your partner expects in bed.

1. HE HOPES YOU ARE PREPPED:

Men like it when their partner is prepared for sex. You make his day when you arrive with a condom, not that the one in his wallet is useless. They are glad when you take responsibility for your sexual health, it shows your own personal maturity.

2. TELL HIM WHAT YOU WANT:

Your partner is not psychic. Men often wonder whether they are doing all right. So tell him what you want and take the guessing game out of the equation. You can voice your intentions in many different ways. A subtle touch one-way, a caress, telling him … hey Ladies … you do not need me to show you how.

3. GIVE YOUR CONSENT:

The adage "Playing hard to get" is on your partner's mind if you consistently turn him down for sex. Cat and mouse games will be the last thing he is interested in when it comes to sex. He will be interested in the here and now. In these days of political correctness and sexual harassment, it is easy to get the lines blurred when a rejected lover forces themselves on lovers. Schedule a time or place, but let him wonder about your intentions. Keep him hanging and eager, but do not give him a definite "No" or "Yes".

4. YOU HAVE TO WANT IT:

We all want and need sex and we all want our partner to be in the mood too. Men traditionally initiates the art of lovemaking, and unless, they are sex addicts, rapists or maniacs, they require that their significant other would be eager to get on with the deed, otherwise they'll think their partner is not into them. Spring some surprise sex gymnastic onto him or her and you'll be loved more for it.

5. PRAISE HIM:

In between the cruel day of hard work and life's other little obligations, praise is the last thing a person expects to hear. At a time when he feels that nothing is going right for him and he wants to give up, spread some cheer his way. Be enthusiastically supportive and let him know he is doing right, especially when in bed. He will appreciate it more, knowing that he is doing the right thing instead of being censured, as he has been all day.

6. EXHIBIT FOR HIM:

Your spouse appreciates your beauty especially your body. Even if you think your body is less than perfect with those stretch marks, fat tummy and that mole. To him or her, your body is a sphinx to them. Let him look at it to his hearts content. It shows your intimacy and openness with him. It's the same effect when he sees you in that special lingerie of yours. He is appreciating the gift beneath the packaging.

7. BE NOISY:

Your partner will not like making love to a turnip. Silent, dry and barely moving. Guys expect their partners to be vivacious and passionate or at least make a moan or breathe heavily when they are fucking. Men don't like the silence. They need to know they are doing a passable job pleasing their lover. A couple of soft moans and "oh yeah" when he touches your G-spot will alleviate his fears.

8. REVEL IN THE FOREPLAY:

All men enjoy foreplay. It takes time for some men, not all, to be ready for the act of lovemaking. So they delight in the slow build-up and tantalising symmetry of fondling. So take the initiative, tease, and whisper your desires to him, slowing the bedroom antics down to a pace both of you are comfortable with.

9. SAY HIS NAME:

Crooning or screaming his name in the throes of passion makes your man feel like he is King Kong. A King of the Hill. They love it. It is a huge turn-on for them. If in throes of fervour, you mistakenly cry out the name of an ex, then missy, a *"New York Minute"* will not be fast enough to watch him disappear and/or lose interest in you.

10. TALK NASTY TO HIM:

Your partner knows you are not a prune but he would not mind if you act and talked like a slut sometimes. Whisper some degenerating slutty words in his ear before he fills the gas tank or before he leaves for work. It would pique his interest and nag at him for the rest of the day until he sees you. I tell you the sex that night would be …. Wow …. Yes, men love it when their partner gets damn right nasty and *"Dirrty"* with them.

11. BE IMPULSIVE AND ADVENTURESOME:

Guys, even some girls want to share their fantasies with their lovers, but worry their partners will shame or judge them. Okay, you both enjoy the Missionary position but after a while, it is bound to be boring. Have an open conversation with him and promise not to find fault with one another. Ascertain if you both will be willing to try other positions or perhaps try having sex at different locations, times or maybe add a little kink to your love life, say a dildo or handcuffs. Make an honest effort to fulfil his fantasy and he will no doubt want to do the same for you.

What Not To Say To A Woman.

Here are some phrases that are not to be uttered by a man to a girl. Be prepared for their wrath if you even think of these terms when you are around them.

- **"You remind me of my mother"**

    No girl wants to be reminded of anyone's mother. Especially not an aging fifty year old.

- **"Are you gonna wear that?"**

    Well she was going to until just then. Oh great, Congratulations. Now you will not only have to wait another couple of hours for her to find another outfit, your day is ruined. Best of luck of getting *"any"* after that.

- **"You look tired"**

    Ha ha. Yeah, good of you for noticing. Yes, I am fucking tired. Tired of every Tom, Dick, and Harriet reminding me that I'm grossed out and that I have bags the size of India under my eyes.

- **"Oomph ... Your sis is Hot!"**

    What the hell is wrong with you? How very repellent. Now you're implying she got short changed in the gene pool.

- **"You have a very pretty face"**

    Just my face huh? Ha. So what! You made it past my neck and decided the rest of me was hideous?

- **"Hey don't take this the wrong way, but …"**

No? Well how else are they supposed to take it now?

- **"Don't be angry, I was kidding"**

Oh yeah, that was funny. Like … you know super funny. Jack Ass.

- **"Calm Down"**

Me? I am Calm. But you are making it so extremely difficult for me to stay calm.

- **"Is it that time of the month, again?"**

Hells no, but I might as well be now after that remark. I should stab you in the eye.

- **"You still hungry?"**

I wasn't before. Now, you know what? I'm gonna inhale this foot long subway and not feel bad about it

- **"You might be able to fit in this"**

Are you mentally retarded or something? *Might*! What in hell's inferno do you mean by "might"?

- **"It's not you, it's me"**

Yeah. Nice one. We'll leave it at that.

- **Please don't freak out"**

Freak out??? Me, freaking out? Do you really wanna see me freak out?

- **Didn't you wear that yesterday?"**

    Oh yeah ... so ...? What are you gonna do about it?

- **"You're bat-shit crazy"**

    Hmmm ... If I were in fact crazy, it would be a very terrible idea to tell me that ... wouldn't it?

- **"You ask a lot of questions"**

    Maybe if you fuckin' learned to answer them correctly I wouldn't have to ask so frickin' many.

- **"How much do you weigh?"**

    Huh? You guessed it. Not worth an explanation

What do Men like in women?

- ❖ Not all Men are romantics at heart. Even if she says she does not like a sense of allure, some part of her is enticed by the notion, particularly in in public. Guys, try their best to be romantic even if they can't pull it off. At times, they can and their lover appreciates his endeavours. They love the effort especially if it is associated with a surprise. Surprises that are not tethered to special occasions.
- ❖ When a woman compliments an item of clothing that their partner wears, it is best to take the verbal cue and wear it more.
- ❖ Women like it when their partner asks advice from them. It shows that there is trust in the relationship and that she is someone you can count on.

What Men do not like:

- Guys despise dramatic women – Drama Queens - who love to create storms a teacups. The use of tears is a formidable weapon in such a woman's arsenal. It helps them seem very convincing.
- Comparing your spouse to any other man can result in a catastrophic domestic event. There is a real existential element to that comparison. It could make any man feel insecure.
- Some men like some women are great manipulators. They lie, cheat, betray, treat you badly and somehow manage to make it all seem like your fault. Don't fall for it, neither should you believe them. IT IS NOT YOUR FAULT.
- Men do not like partners who are insecure. Insecure of themselves and their relationships. Partners who think of themselves of little worth. Not worth the attention of her companion or her friends. They question themselves about their feelings, his or her companions taste in partners, even their taste in lovers.
- No one likes being the second fiddle in his or her partner's lives. Men are especially very cautious of their lovers who are not exactly over their Ex.
- Men do not like women who have learned the art of beneficial nagging. As far as men are concerned, women are not rational twenty-five percent of any given time. All they hear during that counterproductive time is *"yak … yak … yak … yak …"*. Those are the times he feels vehemently lethargic and dreams about his long-since-gone bachelor days. The days he doesn't have to explain his frustration, that broken lamp, the pulling of his hair or that punched hole in wall.
- Most men abhor female *"Rabble-rousers"* or as more eloquently put by a mate, *"Troublemakers"*. Women who cannot, for the love of God and all that's holy, let things go, because she does not like it. These sorts of women argue

loudly and heatedly in front of everyone, not caring about embarrassment. Herself and especially her partner. She argues intensely believing her problems could be solved by being cantankerous and argumentative.
- Men get very circumspect of women who have any kind of a psychological instability. They fear they will get "Fatal Attracted" on for their mistake.
- Most men can stand women who are unsympathetic when it comes to showing compassion. They cannot intuitively feel the presence of a cold heart but can see the effects. Some men will choose to ignore or be on the guarded side if the woman they are interested in has a more than beautiful figure.
- Among the worst complainers are women who are almost neurotic when it comes to matters of the heart and behaviourisms. Men can't abide untrusting women.

What Men Are Keen On:

Men require from their partners a beneficial baseline for a healthy relationship. He needs to know that his life will be unshackled, freed from boredom and that you love him unreservedly. Beyond that, his other needs add value to your relationship.

Here are some points your partner may need or may require you to take note.

- Guys like their own space. Usually when a girlfriend hears her boyfriend demand "space" she immediately thinks the relationship is in crisis mode. That is almost not the case. Men at required times, demand alone time to process their thoughts and feelings.
- Men love sex, however it doesn't mean they are always up for it. He literally does not get a hard-on on the drop of a dime. Sometimes, he may have to be primed or seek aid. Be it, that little blue pill or your gentle caress. Put pressure on him to

perform and he might just lose the inclination to perform, not to mention his erection.
- Men will go to great lengths to avoid asking for help. It is a matter of pride. Don't rely on them when it comes to navigating to your favourite camping site.
- If it is a guy thing, then he must be good at it. If he's not, he does not expect or want you to ever ask him about it.
- Most men suffer from performance anxiety whenever they are force to accept defeat in the bedroom. They can accept their favourite team's defeat but not theirs. Not when it comes to the bedroom.
- Guys hate being chastised by their partners, especially in public.
- Some men are great manipulators. They lie, cheat, betray, treat you badly and somehow manage to make it all seem like your fault. Don't fall for it, neither should you believe them. **IT IS NOT YOUR FAULT.**
- Some women create rumours. These are Haters. They spread their rumours and use fools to spread them, which in turn are accepted by idiots.
- Men do not enjoy their partners making fun of his hobbies and friendships. They are not always a threat to their partners. It is preferable to support and encourage his healthy sporting outlets. It provides a necessary balance for both partners.
- Some guys are not usually big talkers or are not quick to communicate what is up with them, compared to women.
- Guys love encouragement. They love it when their partners think of them as their number one fan. They need that encouragement because in every man's heart are those answers that plaques all men "Is this all I can be?" or "Do I have what it takes?" On the whole, guys need to be instilled with this confidence especially from their partners. Guys perform better when their partner encourages them to do so.

- What does your partner do for excitement? There must be an element of fun in every man's life and his definition of fun might be completely different from yours. Then again, here is something you should know. Men love adventures. You cannot go wrong with men when it comes to exciting activities.
- Men do not like partners who are not over the Ex or who are friends with that "special" male friend.
- Love at first sight is necessarily true, at least when it comes to men. Guys are first attracted to the physical qualities of a girl before anything else. Some men have their preferences. A woman's feet, her smile, the appearance of dimples, her eyes, anything that takes his fancy.
- Once a guy, can make a girl reach that tempestuous rapture of orgasm, the more powerful he feels. The longer you orgasm or the more frequent, the prouder he will feel and the more appreciation he will have for you. However, there is an inverse occurrence where you orgasm and then, you wholly own belong to him.
- Men undoubtedly will take a snapshot of a beautiful woman's cleavage when she isn't looking, no matter his protestations. They cannot help themselves. It is a man thing.
- Men, from a young age are very curious of the female anatomy, hence their porn stash. Even when married to a wonderful person and living happily, his porn stash will not be far from him. Do not hate him for that, it is just his natural inquisitiveness at play. It's harmless.
- It is an authentic fact that all men desire to be the envy of many chicks. It is one of those fantasies that have been imbedded into their brains since our prehistoric days. Their top five most perfect fantasies is to be mobbed by girls in tiny bikinis on a beach. On the other hand, preferably in a nudist colony.
- Men just adore sweet cute shy girls who turn out to be a holy terror in the sack.

Before the "I Dos" & Other Compendiums

- It is not every day that a man receives compliments. When they do, specifically from a girl they have a desire for they feel over the moon. It is a gesture he is not likely to stop thinking about anytime soon.
- It is a peculiar abstract but Guys love girl on girl action. They are turned on by having girls go down on each other. Some guys do not even think that their girlfriend kissing another girl is cheating. They see it as a "green-light" for a *ménage à tour* action.
- Even if they don't say it often enough Men truly love their partners. Men are not vociferous when it comes to saying sappy things girls like to hear. They do try to demonstrate their mind-sets through actions. It's their most secure way of saying "I Love U"
- The way to a man's heart is through his stomach. It is not bad advice for a great adage. A well-prepared meal will send his tummy in spins with adoration for you.
- Men like to be told things straight. Do not say something that means something else.
- It takes a while, but men do stray into another relationship if the partner of the house does not meet their psychological, physical, and emotional needs.
- Men don't like to be manipulated even if they are easy to manoeuvre.
- To take control of any relationship with a man, it is advisable to show him the respect he deserves. That is the sweetest craving a man will need. Do that and he will be under your thumb, loving you more and more.

What Do His Actions or Thoughts Mean?

- When a guy suddenly stops in a crowd or on a street, it might be because an attractive girl has just accidently brushed passed him and he had an uncontrollable turn on. As by

evidence of his stiffened cock within his pants covered flimsy by his briefcase or rucksack.
- If a man is still in love with someone else, he'll always defend her but deny his involvement with her.
- If he pretends he can't hear you, it only means they are involved with something else. It is a man's way of getting out of a useless argument or unrelenting nagging or something else.
- When he seems thoughtful, it is because men find it hard to remember even the littlest things.
- It takes more than the male instinct to know when a woman is interested in them.
- If a man really cares about someone, you will see it in his smile.

What Women Like In the Bedroom:

Arousal is the name of the game and it has a dual function. Green light and Red. Different people like different things. We all differ when it comes to activating our sexual accelerators and when it comes time to hit red light. Fortunately, science and our inner selves are partly responsible for the means to do both. In any case, despite societies teaching of restraint, we find that despite protestations our partners desire what we want behind the closed doors of the bedroom. Yes, some partners are interested in nipple wax, whips, and rings most are in interested in having a sexual adventure. Relationships work better if partners exceed their comfort zone and explore their needs. Here are some thoughts about what your female partner may expect in bed.

1. **SHE HOPES FOR PLEASURE & YOU TO TREAT HER WITH RESPECT - LIKE A SEX GODDESS:**

    Women want pleasure by any appropriate means necessary, but it's inbuilt in men that he doesn't expect you to be perfect until you perform in bed. He expects you to be just okay in bed, but hopes you are better than his previous girlfriends put together. The trick is to be pleasure specific. If you are flirty or sexy then maybe tickling your G-spot is your poison or your innocuous nooky. You have to expect him to facilitate pleasure any way he can. If he cannot, it is not a bad idea to guide him. Let him touch you in a way that gives you pleasure. Any feeling, including pain can be perceived as pleasure oriented. It is all in the context. Whether he uses a soft stress reaction or high-stylised affection to create pleasure, you hope it matches your pleasure threshold. He might not be perfect but at least you will have great sex.

2. SLAVE OR MASTER or BOTH:

Some women demand more or less, depending on the circumstance. They need someone who could remove all stressors. A protector, a pleasurer, breadwinner, everything. Someone who will take her to the country club in the morning, take her shopping in the afternoon and buy hey a convertible and then return home where he will tie her to the boot and fuck her ten ways from Sunday in the evening. What woman wouldn't want that? Someone to remove all nervous tension and the constant worry. Someone who she can trust with her body and mind so completely she feels safe to let life be set on cruise control.

Hey, hold on. There are not many relationships like this and it should be noted that except from couples in Orange County and others, for the man's interest in playing the dominant figure in this relationship, the woman has to know her partners restraint before she will allow this rapport.

3. SHE HOPES YOU ARE PAYING ATTENTION:

Your partner is not clairvoyant. Men or women often wonder whether they are doing all right. So tell him or her what you want and take the guessing game out of the equation. You can voice your intentions in many different ways. A subtle touch one-way, a caress, telling him ... hey Ladies ... you do not need me to tell you how.

4. SHE DOES NOT NEED YOU STRESSING:

She does not want you to be stressed about your performance, especially the first time. You are both nervous and eager, it is only understandable her nerves are easily hidden and his shows as an aneroid barometer of penis anxiety. Granted, first time sex is always froth with highly charged expectations but she does expect it to be at least passionately and perceptively erotic. If his nervousness will causes a lack of erection or he prematurely ejaculates, her reaction will set the tone on how good the sex between both of you might be in the future. If she does not make a big deal out of it, you are set for an open honest and communicative sex in the future. If she overreacts then its goodbye sunshine. Goodbye sunshine, because he will definitely take it personally and be more apprehensive the next time around.

5. PRAISE & INGRATIATE YOURSELF TO HER:

After a hard day of work and fulfilling life's other little responsibilities, compliment is the last thing she expects to hear from anyone. At a time when she feels that nothing is going right for her and she wants to give up, spread some cheer her way. Do not necessarily wait to be told what she wants and like. Be unreservedly supportive in a way that allows her to feel galvanised and self-assured. Show your understanding of her as no one else does because she wants to know if you really see her and only her. See her with a single-mindedness that only focuses on her and let her know that despite everything she has you to count on. At home

Before the "I Dos" & Other Compendiums

and especially in bedroom, she will be pleased about it more, knowing that things are going her way at least for now.

6. AT TIMES, SHE TENDS TO BE VIVACIOUS:

You are shy and conservative. He gets that. However, in the sack, you become an animalistic version of yourself. It is a surprise but it is just what the doctor ordered and what your partner has been waiting to see. Men appreciate fucking a wildcat. They need to know their partner is alive and as excitable as they are and that they are pleasing their partner as opposed to a routinely sex act that is dull and as exciting as a discarded old paint can. A couple of screaming cries of pleasure when he caresses her G-spot will encourage his unrelenting fuckathon.

7. CONFIDENCE & YOUR FOREPLAY SESSION:

Not all women enjoy foreplay. They prefer to get the business of sex over and done with. Alternatively, they hope you are confident to know what you are doing. So take the initiative, tease, but do not prolong your actions because what may be true about your body may not be true about your partner's body. Confidence is knowing what is true about yours and his body. Not all bodies are the same. A characteristic that is only learned by teaching and practice. For example, an insecure partner criticises a woman for wanting what she wants and liking what she likes and for doing the things she has done or for having the notions and sentiments, she has. Do not forget, your desires are what he needs to fulfil and by extension his. You need to communicate your feelings about what you like, what you want, and what you would like to try. As an opener, you may mutually choose the bedroom antics to a pace you are comfortable with. Learn to appreciate each other's bodies and sexualities it's the first thing women appreciates. It may make men feel like they are being worshiped.

8. **BE ACTIVELY JOYOUS:**

   Our bodies contain certain peculiarities that we should be Joyous about or not. We learn to be joyously true of our sexuality and our bodies. It is not all that easy at times. Not all of our bodies match with our sexuality because we are taught early in life at home or by the tabloids that we are not synchronically compatible. We are all the time, discovering and re-experiencing that our bodies are gorgeous and powerful precisely just as they are. Do not be concerned, your partner really wants you to be joyful about their body.

   Women need and want to feel good, be safe and protected. They are not that complicated. They understand themselves and know they want to be the object of intense, specific desire from any man. It is nothing new, it is just a universal female craving. Uncomplicated yes, but not always, especially in a society where women are told daily that they are damaged, ruined, and unlovable.

9. **KEEP IT SIMPLE:** You wanting to impress her is one thing, but trying to squeeze half of the erogenous positions you are familiar with, does quite the opposite.

10. **CALL OUT HER NAME:**

    Whispering her name in her ears while in the throes of passion makes your woman feel like she is Doris Day or Miss World. She loves it. It is a huge turn-on for them. Half way through your sex-ergonomics, he might leave it up to you to make all the moves and calls.

11. BE NASTY TO HER:

Hard orgasmic sex is very exhaustingly cool but at times, you need a motivator. A stimulus in the form of your frustration. Not at her, but it would be good to take it out on her or being down right dirty and nasty. Your partner knows you are not a prune but she would not mind if you acted tough and bore savagely into her sometimes. She might expect you to impart some expletive blasphemous words at her while you hammer into her with all your might.

12. WILLING TO BE ADVENTUROUS:

It is not every guy's favourite thing to do but if she wants oral sex, you are willing to let her experiment. She expects to be orgasmic tingling all over after this, so make an honest effort to fulfil her fantasies and she will no doubt want to do the same for you.

What Women do not Like In the Bedroom:

Not everyone is conducive to sex. Some partners cannot bear some others. They hope to say something but they never do. They should. Some women are agreeable to sex for recreation, some relaxation, others procreation, depending on the individual. Here are some thoughts about what your female partner may not want in bed.

1. THE FACE YOU PULL:

If you're on top and she's just staring at you, what do you think of? What your face is saying or what's she thinking. Do you just close your eyes and carry on?

2. ASKING QUESTIONS:

Asking *"Do you like that?"* or *"How do you want it?"* is very distracting and unnecessary. If you're doing a good or bad job, she is unlikely to tell you. Her expression and body writhes should be more than enough to tell you if you're doing a good job. Besides, she'll instinctively tell you what she likes. If she's keen on a certain position or not.

3. RECREATION:

She wouldn't like you recreating some sexual position you saw online without her input. Or be so great at a sexual position with you having practiced on her. She will wonder, "How did you get so good without her?"

4. THE CONDOM SNAFU:

She doesn't like asking you to put your condom on or how to put it on. You should already know or come fully suited and prepared without prompting from her.

5. WHEN YOU JUST STOP:

She hates it when you just stop in the middle, especially when she's having the time of her life. Hey, everyone hates that. Even in the middle of an orgasm. It's like *"Hey! What the hell, Did I orgasm? No"*

6. SIXTY-NINE:

He wants to do a 69 and insists to be on top. Yak! You basically suffocate under him with his weight and his face.

7. CLEANLINESS:

His baggy short stinks and taste of urine. Eww! You do not want to remove his dirty, smelly shorts with your teeth. His stubble is dirty and the wrong type on his face. On the other hand, feeding your face with fried chicken before a blowjob on uncircumcised drenched urine. Eww!! Holy Christ, it the worst taste imaginable.

8. ROUGH FOREPLAY:

He puts his fingers everywhere or being aggressive with his hands during foreplay or thinks it is a good idea to stick sex toys in you, as if sorting out which to play an orchestral. Or he tries to casually stick his cock into your arse without consent or using some lubricant. Hey, even nipple biting or hair pulling is off-putting. It all just fucking hurts.

What Not To Say To A Man.

Here are some phrases and suggestions that are not to be uttered by a girlfriend/fiancé to her partner. That is unless you want him to be infuriated with you. Be prepared for his wrath if you even think of them when you are around him.

- **"You remind me of my Ex"**

    Yeah, cool. So you dated other guys before him. Who wants to be reminded or compared to someone else, especially an ex.

- **Don't pester him**

    Every time you spend time with him, try not to tell him he needs to change a specific event or feature. Choose your battles wisely. Err on the side of adding value to him.

- **"I'm Fine"**

    Hell, you are not fine. Something is bothering you, so tell him about it. He doesn't like hearing it, that doesn't mean he doesn't want to hear about what is bothering you.

- **"If you loved me, you would know"**

    Guys don't like being teased with tests.

- **"You have a small dick anyway"**

    Jokes are jokes. This is not one of them. He does not care if you are quarrelling. It makes him completely self-conscious. How would you like it if he told you, "You are fat"

- **"Do you think she is pretty?"**

Tell the truth. You don't really want to know the truth, do you? He knows you are setting him up for failure. It's just callous and a little Machiavellian.

- **"When we are married …"**

Guys hate to talk about commitment until they are good and ready. Five to six weeks of dating doesn't qualify for the discussion of marriage. It's probable he'll get scared and run off, no matter how much he fancies you.

- **"Who texted you?"**

What the hell? He's allowed to get text messages without you looking over his shoulder. Stop spying on him.

- **"Aren't these condoms too big for you?"**

Jesus. What are you trying to do? Question his manhood? Never question a man's girth to his face. Men tend to immature and self-conscious about their body. Question his penis and you just might destroy his confidence in all things.

- **"You don't really know how to change a tire, do you?"**

Instinctively, all men know how to change a tire. Those who do not, do not need it pointed out to them.

- **"I don't like your friends"**

There is honesty and there's just being malicious and being inconsiderate. Unless you have a very legitimate reason, try not to be hostile to your partner's boys. They (No matter how intolerable) made him into the person you love, don't forget that.

PREMARITAL QUERY LISTS

The triumph or disaster of your marriage relationship depends on how well you handle a number of personal issues. Here are some questions that you need to review with your other half.

1. RELATIONSHIP OBJECTIVES & PERSONAL ROUTINES

- Is your relationship going to change after your marriage?
- What do you as a couple want out of life?
- Why are you getting married?
- What do you think you both will be doing in thirty or forty years?
- Have you ever hit someone?
- How would you describe yourself?
- Do you have a criminal record?
- How often do you drink?
- How do you think your significant other sees you?
- Will you help clean the toilet?
- Does religion play an important part in your life?
- Do you think faith and spirituality are important in a marriage?
- Do you believe in God and What is your image of God?

2. ECONOMICS

- Are you a gatherer or paymaster when it comes to money?
- Do you ever talk about money?
- How much do you owe in debts and what are your assets?
- Where does your money go?
- Should you have a joint checking account or separate accounts or both?
- Who is going to be responsible for paying the bills?
- Do you consider going to the movies and having a vacation every year a necessity or a luxury?

- What are our future plans for purchasing a home?
- Do we both know where our important financial documents are located?

3. FAMILY

- Do you want to have children?
- How long should you be married before having children?
- What kind of parent do you think you both will be?
- How many children do you want to have?
- What was your childhood like?
- What will be your parenting viewpoint?
- Will one of you stay home after you have children?
- How do you feel about adoption?
- Do you have children already?
- What values do you want to bring from your family into our marriage?
- What do you like and dislike about your family?
- What do you like and dislike about your partners family?
- How much time will you both spend with your in-laws?

4. SEX & INTIMACY

- Do you talk about sex?
- Are you both comfortable discussing your sexual predilections?
- Do I have trust issues or feel insecure?
- What are your expectations of your sexual relationship?
- Are you a jealous person?
- How important are affirmations to me?
- Compliments, how well do you handle them?
- How will you describe love language?
- Do you think you both are good conversationalists?
- Do you think it is important to be faithful to one another?
- How do you want to spend our days off?

- Do you believe you both should be doing everything together?
- Do you both pursue your own interests?
- Do you take personal time-outs?
- How would you feel if I want a night out with my friends now and then?
- Should we plan our quality time together?

5. DISPUTES & INTERACTIONS

- Should we both be willing to face difficult situations or do we try to avoid conflict?
- Do you think we have problems in our relationship that we counselling before our wedding?
- Do you handle conflict well?
- How will you make decisions together?
- How are you different?
- Do you think your differences will create problems in your marriage?
- Do you expect or want to change?
- Can you be forgiven if the unexpected happened?
- Are you both willing to work on your communication skills and share intimately with each other?

DEGREES OF SEPARATION:

"Everything we hear is an opinion, not a fact. Everything we see is a perspective, not the Truth" – Marcus Aurelius.

Is An Amicable Breakup Possible?

Songs have been sung, poems have been written, and paintings have been drawn all for the sake of a love lost. We all wish for things to work out for the best. Nonetheless, conditions, emotions, and circumstances do change. Circumstances can be poisonous or revitalised nectar. Most of us lose ourselves in love. It's not something to be ashamed about. The hitch is that despite your broken heart you do not get lost in your own misery. More and more times in today's social order, we see increasing adversarial constrictions related to breakups. So is a clean break-up possible? I believe there is a breakup where there are no lingering resentments. I could be wrong but hey, what do I know.

Here are some suggestions on how to apply an amicable separation.

- **Let the arrangements lead the financials:**

    A battle is sure to ensue over entitlements, but if you begin with the small items it can help focus on the priorities of what you may feel you deserve when it comes to the financial aspects of your lives together.

- **Let the past be the past:**

    Discussion with your ex-spouse will at all times be tough. Therefore, it will be necessary to be emotionally ready. Try not to think of that time in the past when he or she forgot to dry the dishes, got you two lost on that vacation in Italy or forgot that anniversary two years ago. Resists the old and accept the end of things. The future is here, anew and full of curious occurrences. This idea means that the past should be just that, the past.

- **If conceivable plan the break up:**

If at all possible, try and plan the break-up, it should give you both time to process your feelings. Discuss your feelings and ask all the questions you never wanted to ask before the farewells.

- **Try to be as candid and open as you can be:**

Try to inform him or her why this is a necessary step for you. Be open and truthful, not vague and ambiguous. Let him or her know that you were not getting something from the relationship. If you do not, there would be a feeling of resentment and distrust thrown your way.

- **Discuss the kind of relationship you want to go forward with:**

It is plausible that you feel that time apart might give you both a clear perspective of the relationship. Maybe you feel smothered or unappreciated in the relationship and that either of you might not be able to progress fully to their full potential in light of such a liaison. Let your partner know in clear details how much time apart might be needed, if at all. There is no objective in creating hope where there might not be one.

- **Purge all Contact:**

Social media is the bane of relationships in our time. It is best you purge all contact links with your former partner. Everything in Facebook, Twitter etc. Stay away from social media for a while. It will prevent you from making a fool of yourself by making unnecessary twitter or SMS exchanges.

- **Control Your Grief:**

    Do not act tough. You are mourning, take the time to feel it. There is no use in hiding your emotions. Those close to you will know you are hurting. Feel the flood of emotions, if you need to shed some tears, then go ahead. You are mourning the death of a relationship and like any real death, you have to go through the five stages of grief. Anger, repudiation, bargaining, despair, and acceptance. After a while, it won't hurt so much, at that time dust yourself off and return to the world.

- **Learn from the Experience:**

    You cannot turn back time, but you can definitely learn from the mistakes you have made and the time you put into your failed relationship.

- **Take Responsibility:**

    It may not be your fault that your relationship failed but for a harmonious separation, you should own your part in it. It takes two to tango, so it is not completely the other partner whose fault you have to go your separate ways.

- **Accept support from your Loved Ones:**

    Inform your older and wiser relation or friend on what has transpired. No matter what ails you, I bet he or she will help you to feel better and remind you of your tremendous value. Have them watch over you while you cry in your ice cream or drown your sorrows with alcohol. They love you and will not judge you (At least they should not) as you cry on their shoulders.

- **Show your Qualities:**

    What about yourself is worthy of the life you lead. There must be at least five worthy attributes that could materialise from you in a positive way. Remind yourself repeatedly that someone else appreciates you and that you can make your way through life's ups and down.

- **Rediscover yourself:**

    Find a new hobby that would please you. Change your look. Dust off those old classics. Its time you reinvent your self-worth.

- **Persevere:**

    There are plenty of fishes in the sea. He or she is not the only person out there who wouldn't appreciate you. You will find that person, it is just a matter of being patient.

The "Don'ts" when breaking up a relationship:

Under no circumstances should you do the following after a break up.

- **Don't have Break-up Sex:**

    You broke up for a reason and you've been making a solid effort to get over him or her. Why complicate it? Your defences will be lowered and your serotonin levels will spike with an empathy reaction, leading you back to the emotional state you were before you broke up. Best when you two meet up, you think with your brain and not your heart or genitals.

- **Move on too quickly:**

Yes, you are in a fragile place and suddenly you are chatting up some Adonis or some babe in a bikini wear. What to do? Of course, you go for it. It is a bad idea. Yes, you are desperate to feel wanted by anybody but it is unfair to drag another person into your fragile mess. Technically, this will be a rebound relationship and your lone goal will be to show off. Especially to your ex, signalling them that you can cope with their input. Do not bet on it. This action will probably leave you in a worse emotional state than before.

- **Don't insult your ex's family or friends:**

Bad humour or resentment is not a good look on anybody. It leaves a sour taste in the wake of that individual. Keep comments about your ex short and generalised. Avoid sliding into that dark place where the outcome could much more deliberate than you imagine.

- **Don't substance abuse:**

There is not a technology yet that can plug that hole in your heart. Naturally, some of us tend to veer towards an easier solution. Naturally, drugs or alcohol. Alcohol is a poor man's sedative while narcotic drugs take some of us down a very slippery downward slope. If you have to drown your sorrows, then do it in moderation. The future does look bleak indeed but time heals all wounds as well as break ups.

GUIDANCE QUESTIONS

Considering That Church Wedding?

1. Where can I get married if I'm not baptised or I don't go to church? Can I still get married in a church?
2. How do I book a Church?
3. Can I get married in any Church?
4. Is a church blessing possible if I want to get married abroad?
5. Can I still get married in a church if I'm divorced?
6. What are the legal requirements?
7. Why do we need legal or marriage preparation?
8. How much will all this cost? I'm not exactly rich.
9. Do we need two rings or one?
10. Can we marry in any other colour besides black and white?
11. What if one of us is a foreign national?

MARRIAGE IN THE UNITED STATES.

Marriage laws in the United States are fundamental rights but established by individual states. There two basic methods of recognising a marriage. A Common Law marriage and a marriage requiring a Marriage Licence.

Common Law Marriages are not recognised by most states, while a Marriage that provides for the rights and responsibilities of a married couple, just requires a Marriage Licence, which only needs to be registered in the nearest Town Hall.

COMPARATIVE Q & A

1) How much does he or she tell you she loves you?

    A. Never
    B. Once a day
    C. All the time...every second.
    D. Every once in awhile
    E. When his or her friends aren't around

2) When he or she is around you and his or her friends what does he or she do?

    A. Talks to them and to me too.
    B. We don't hang out with his or her friends.
    C. Just talks to them.
    D. Leaves me by myself until they're gone and then comes and talks to me
    E. Only Talks to me

3) When you talk what do you talk about?

    A. Me
    B. How much we miss each other
    C. General topics
    D. Him
    E. Everything...things we both like

4) Do you love her or him?

    A. Maybe
    B. I don't know yet
    C. *sigh* yes but I don't want him or her to know
    D. YES!
    E. No

5) How much time do you spend together?

   A. Everyday
   B. Only on Weekends
   C. Only when he or she wants to have sex.
   D. Once a month
   E. Once a week

6) When you are together what do you do?

   A. Just Hang out
   B. Make love...Do it
   C. Talk ... Hug and kiss... make love...hangout
   D. Talk
   E. Hug and kiss... make love

7) Do you see yourself with him or her for the rest of your lives?

   A. I could imagine it.
   B. Yes… Absolutely
   C. I don't even want to begin... it's just sex or convenience sake
   D. No
   E. I don't think I want to.

8) How long have you been with him or her?

   A. A month
   B. We're not together!
   C. A couple days
   D. A year or more
   E. Almost a month

9) Is very supportive of things that I do.
   ○ Yes   No ○

10) Encourages you to try new things.
    ○ Yes   No ○

11) Likes to listen when I have something on my mind.
    ○ Yes   No ○

12) Understands that you have your own life too.
    ○ Yes   No ○

13) Is not liked my friends.
    ○ Yes   No ○

14) Says I'm too involved in different activities.
    ○ Yes   No ○

15) Texts me or calls me all the time.
    ○ Yes   No ○

16) Thinks I spend too much time trying to look nice.
    ○ Yes   No ○

17) Gets extremely jealous or possessive.
    ○ Yes   No ○

18) Accuses me of flirting or cheating.
    ○ Yes   No ○

19) Constantly checks up on me or makes me check in.
    ○ Yes   No ○

20) Controls what I wear or how I look.
    ○ Yes   No ○

21) Tries to control what I do and who I see.
   ◯ Yes   No ◯

22) Tries to keep me from seeing or talking to my family and friends.
   ◯ Yes   No ◯

23) Has big mood swings - gets angry and yells at me one minute, but is sweet and apologetic the next.
   ◯ Yes   No ◯

24) Puts me down, calls me names or criticizes me.
   ◯ Yes   No ◯

25) Makes me feel like I can't do anything right or blames me for problems.
   ◯ Yes   No ◯

26) Makes me feel like no one else would want me.
   ◯ Yes   No ◯

27) Threatens to hurt me, my friends or family.
   ◯ Yes   No ◯

28) Threatens to hurt him or herself because of me.
   ◯ Yes   No ◯

29) Threatens to destroy my things.
   ◯ Yes   No ◯

30) Makes me feel nervous or like I'm "walking on eggshells."
   ◯ Yes   No ◯

31) Grabs, pushes, shoves, chokes, punches, slaps, holds me down, throws things or hurts me in some way.
   ◯ Yes   No ◯

32) Breaks things or throws things to intimidate me.
   ○ Yes   No ○

33) Yells, screams or humiliates me in front of other people.
   ○ Yes   No ○

34) Pressures or forces me into having sex or going farther than I want to.
   ○ Yes   No ○

COMPARATIVE ANSWERS

1. B
2. C
3. D or C
4. A
5. C
6. B
7. B
8. Y
9. Y
10. Y
11. Y
12. Y
13. Y
14. N
15. N
16. N
17. N
18. N
19. N
20. N
21. N
22. N
23. N
24. N
25. N
26. N
27. N
28. N
29. N
30. N
31. N
32. N
33. N

ANSWERS TO CHURCH WEDDING ETIQUETTE

1. Everyone in England lives in some sort of parish with a parish church. As far as baptism goes, it really depends on your Parish Priest or Vicar or Reverend.

2. Get in contact with your nearest Parish church and speak to your vicar or priest for more information about getting married.

3. Absolutely. The Church of England, not the Catholic Church has explored ways of making it easier for couples to get married in a church outside their parish. At the moment though, if you want to get married in a church that is not your parish church you will need to speak to the minister.

   UK residence could also apply for a Special Licence at;

   The Faculty Office,
   1 The Sanctuary,
   Westminster,
   London
   SW1P 3JT

4. After any civil ceremony, there is a service of prayer and dedication, which can be adapted. So there should not be any reason why this cannot be done. Provided of course you have first discussed it with the Vicar or Priest of your local parish. No legal requirements or fees are required

5. The Church of England believes that marriage is for life. However, it recognises that regrettably, some marriages do fall short. In exceptional circumstances, the Church accepts that a divorced person may marry again. The possibility of

marriage after a divorce depends on the Church's policy and your Priest.

6. Preliminary notice for getting married in the Church of England is by banns. You must be over the age eighteen and you must have your parents' consent to marry. There are circumstances where some form of licence, such as a common licence or a special licence, is much more appropriate. Your vicar should be able to provide you with what you need to do.

   Please Note: that there are special guidelines on a church wedding if you are divorced.

7. All that effort invested in planning your wedding pays off with the fact that the day is an important milestone in your life and should presumably last forever. However, alas as much you both think you know each other, you are still two separate individuals with different backgrounds, temperaments, experiences, aspirations and fears. The legal and marriage preparations are opportunities to formalise and talk through any issues that might arise.

8. Depending on the size of the wedding, your requirements like choir, organist, reception, recording equipment etc. That is up to you. As for the legal marriage cover and publication of the banns, the marriage service and a certificate of marriage it is predominantly between £180 - £260. In the States, it is triple that. In addition, it's non-refundable.

9. It is entirely up to both of you to decide whether you have one ring or two. Your wedding ring is the symbol of your supposedly unending love and faithfulness. A gesture of the life-long commitment you are making to each other.

10. Yes. Definitely.

11. The Church has a responsibility to conduct marriages, which will be recognised in the country the bride or groom comes from. This is not just bureaucracy but for the couple's benefit. If one of the couple is a national of a country outside *Canada, Australia, New Zealand, South Africa, the EU or USA*, then it's not such a problem. Hence, the Faculty Office strongly recommends that these marriages should be done by Common Licence rather than banns, and requires that the couple obtain from the relevant embassy or consulate a recognition letter of their marriage.

Printed in the United States
By Bookmasters